The Grammar Guide

The Grammar Guide

Developing Language Skills for Academic Success

Nancy M. Ackles

Ann Arbor
The University of Michigan Press

Letter to the Student

Dear Student,

As I wrote this text, I made three assumptions:

1. that you already know a lot of English,
2. that you want to attend or are attending college, and
3. that you are an intelligent, capable language learner.

I did not assume

1. that you have studied a lot of grammar or
2. that you feel confident and happy in a grammar class.

I have tried to make the grammar explanations in this book clear and easy to understand, even though this is a book of advanced, complex grammar. This book does not discuss everything there is to know about American English. It does, however, explain the things about English you most need to know as an advanced student who wants to do college work in an English language setting.

If you learned English by listening to and talking with English speakers, you may have learned how to communicate well without paying much attention to small details, and you may not have learned many formal grammar terms. This book will help you learn the details you need for writing well in an academic setting, and the first chapter will help you learn the basic terms used in grammar books.

If you learned English by taking classes and studying grammar books, you may need to pay particular attention to the word partnerships (or *collocations*) in which the vocabulary words are used. Using these phrases will help make your English sound natural.

This is a grammar textbook, so my first goal was to help you with grammar. Of course, for college work, you need to develop your writing skills too, and you will find many topics for discussion and writing in this book. One of the very best ways to prepare for college is to write and write and write some more, and I hope that you will be able to use the writing and discussion topics for lots of practice using English.

In addition, learning a language involves learning vocabulary. In many cases, grammar and vocabulary are very closely tied together. This book will help you increase your academic vocabulary. In 1990, Paul Nation developed the University Word List. This is a list of about 800 words that appear very frequently in academic writing. Nation tried to identify the most important words for academic students to learn after they learn the 2,000 or so most common words in English. In 2000, Nation's colleague Averil Coxhead created an updated list of 570 words called the Academic Word List. I used words from these two lists throughout this text. As you read this book, you will find the majority of the words on the University Word List and 558 of the 570* words on the Academic Word List used at least once in one of their meanings, and many of the words are used much more frequently. The words from these lists used in each chapter can be found in the appendix.

I have tried to use the vocabulary in ways that are natural and that will not cause you problems as you study grammar. For example, the word *assume* is on both the University and the Academic word lists. At the beginning of this letter, I wrote *I made three assumptions* and *I did not assume* and then wrote a list of assumptions. The list helps you know what *assume* and *assumption* mean if you don't already know. The phrase *made three assumptions* is a natural English phrase and demonstrates that the verb *make* is used with *assumptions* and that assumptions are things people count. You should also have a good dictionary, and chapter 1 includes information on dictionaries.

When you see words from the University and Academic word lists, you may notice that you already know the basic meaning of many of the words. If that is true, your goal should be to expand your knowledge of the phrases in which these words appear. Research has shown that advanced language learners often know the basic meanings of words but that native speakers know more about the ways words are usually combined. The schematic diagram that appears in this letter illustrates this situation.

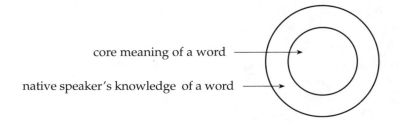

core meaning of a word

native speaker's knowledge of a word

---

*The 12 words that I did not find a place for are *aggregate, behalf, empirical, exploit, hierarchy, invoke, paradigm, parameter, protocol, regime, scenario,* and *sex.*

The words *schematic* (from *scheme*), *diagram, illustrate,* and *core*—used in the preceding paragraph or in the diagram—are all from the word lists, and the diagram can help you see the meaning of these words. If you are not sure of the meaning of *schematic,* you might choose to ignore the word, because you can understand the meaning of the sentence without it. If you choose to study the word, you can be sure that you are not wasting your time. The time that you spend studying the words on the Academic and University word lists is never wasted time because you will see these words again and again as you read for college classes. (A *schematic diagram* is a simple diagram that shows the most important parts of something.)

If a great many of the words from the Academic and University word lists are new to you, you may want to set a weekly goal. For example, you might want to study twenty new words a week. You don't need to do everything at once.

The fictitious first names which are used for people in this text were chosen because they are short (three letters). The names which are used for fictitious corporations were taken from letters of the Greek alphabet.

Every language in the world is very complex, and it is amazing that the human brain can learn even one language. You are mastering two languages, and I salute you.

Nancy Ackles

Letter to the Instructor

Dear Instructor,

This text is intended for advanced bilingual and second language English students. Some of these students have had many years of formal grammar study. Others have learned English by immersion into an English language setting, with limited academic support for their language learning. Many of these students are able to communicate very well but have trouble with academic writing and lack confidence when confronted with grammar books, grammar rules, and grammar tests. I have tried to write clearly for these students while providing explanations that are based on good linguistic research. Because many of these students have lived most of their lives in the United States, I have avoided any discussion questions based on cultural comparison of "your country" versus "our country."

Language has both rules and words. My specialty is syntax, and this is a grammar text, but it will also give students support as they work to increase the range of their vocabulary. It is impossible to predict exactly which words any person will need or want to learn, but students can be confident that time spent learning words from the Academic and University word lists will not be wasted. These are all words that appear again and again in academic writing and are well worth a few minutes of study with a dictionary.

When we know a word well, we know its meaning, but we also know a lot about its "friends and relations." "Relations" are the various forms of the word. "Friends" are the collocations the word often appears in. I have tried to use words from the Academic and University word lists in natural ways with appropriate collocations, so that even if students are not concentrating on vocabulary, they will be exposed to words they will need for their college work and to these words' "friends and relations." Where possible, I have also tried to take into account the information that corpus-based studies are now giving us on which words are used most frequently in various grammatical patterns (such as passive voice).

In my own teaching experience, it has not been uncommon to have in the same classroom an eighteen-year-old student who has not had any college classes yet and a visiting professor doing post-doctoral research. Therefore, I have included a wide range of discussion and writing prompts. Choose the ones that are best for your class. Often, writing 100 or 200 words on a topic is a very productive experience, but every chapter also contains prompts that are appropriate for development into longer, polished essays.

I decided long ago that in a language classroom, the students are the Olympic athletes, and we teachers are merely coaches. I hope that this book will help you as you help your students in this amazing process of learning a language.

Nancy Ackles

Contents

List of Reference Charts

Chapter 1
Tools for Language Learning

Introductory Focus

Consider the following sayings.

> The only place that success comes before work is in the dictionary.
> Of course, with a dictionary and a grammar, a culture is able to protect and defend itself. (Dr. Lamin Sanneh)

Do you have an opinion on the value of studying grammar? Do you have an opinion on the worth of dictionaries?

Metalanguage

Metalanguage is the language we use to talk about language. When you know some metalanguage, you can understand grammar books and dictionaries better and talk to teachers about how to improve your writing. Most people don't want to learn a lot of metalanguage, but learning a little is helpful. This unit will help you with the basic terms you need when you study a language.

Parts of Speech

The ancient Greeks divided Greek words into eight categories and called them *parts of speech*. Although modern linguists say that English words should be divided into more than eight categories, grammar students have used these same eight categories for centuries, and you will find them in most grammar texts, dictionaries, and style guides.

The Eight Traditional Parts of Speech

nouns	Words for things, people, places or ideas. e.g.,[1] *chair, sister, democracy, leisure, stress* My <u>sister</u> is sitting in a <u>chair</u>.
pronouns	Words that are used in place of nouns. e.g., *I, me, you, she, it, them* <u>I</u> gave <u>it</u> to <u>them</u>.
prepositions	Words that begin phrases about location or relationship. e.g., *about, at, from, in, on, of, with, to, under* The museum exhibit is <u>about</u> American history <u>from</u> 1920 <u>to</u> 1945.
verbs	Words that tell an action, experience, or state. e.g., *walk, need, be, exist* Kim <u>walks</u> to school every day. Students often <u>need</u> flexible schedules. A monarch <u>is</u> a king or queen.
adjectives	Words that are used to modify (describe) nouns. e.g., *old, wise, small, efficient* <u>Efficient</u> machines use <u>small</u> amounts of fuel.
adverbs	Words that are used to modify verbs. e.g., *quickly, leisurely, fluently* She writes <u>fluently</u> in English. Words that are used to modify adjectives or adverbs. e.g., *very, really, entirely* He speaks <u>very</u> eloquently. The television program is showing <u>entirely</u> new episodes this season. Words that are used to modify whole sentences. e.g., *fortunately, naturally* <u>Fortunately</u>, the accident occurred near a good medical clinic Words that don't fit into any other category. When the Greeks didn't know what to call a word, they usually called it an adverb; therefore, grammar books often have many special categories of adverbs, such as *conjunctive adverbs* and *correlative adverbs*. The word *not* is usually classified as an adverb.

---

1. *e.g.* stands for the Latin phrase *exempli gratia* and means "for example."

conjunctions	Words that are used to connect words, phrases, or clauses.
	e.g., *and, but, or, nor*
	    We sell domestic <u>and</u> imported cheeses, <u>but</u> we don't sell
	    any kind of alcohol.

interjections	Words and phrases that express sudden feelings. e.g., *Yikes! Ouch! Oh no!*

Notice: In many languages, words have special endings or forms that indicate parts of speech (nouns, verbs, etc.). In English, words sometimes have different forms for different parts of speech and sometimes don't. For example:

Noun	minimum (the smallest amount)	green (a color)
Verb	minimize (make small)	green (become green)
Adjective	minimal (very small)	green (green colored)

There are also some useful subdivisions of these basic parts of speech.

Nouns	
proper nouns	These nouns are names of specific people, places, organizations, etc.[2] Proper nouns are usually written with a capital letter. e.g., *John Smith, Lake Superior, Whitman College*
common nouns	These are all nouns that are not proper nouns. e.g., *man, lake, college, democracy, music, anger*

Pronouns	
subject pronouns	These pronouns can be used as *subjects* in sentences. (See p. 6.) *I, we, you, he, she, it, they* <u>We</u> like ice cream. <u>They</u> like cookies.
object pronouns	These pronouns can be used as *objects*. (See p. 8.) *me, us, you, him, her, it, them* The cat likes <u>me</u>. The dog likes <u>her</u>.
possessive pronouns	These pronouns tell who owns something. *mine, ours, yours, his, hers, theirs* (A few speakers also use *its*.) This book is <u>mine</u>. <u>Yours</u> is on the desk.

---

2. The abbreviation *etc.* stands for the Latin phrase *et cetera* and means "and so on" or "and the rest."

reflexive pronouns	These pronouns are used as objects in sentences when the subject and object are the same individual. *myself, yourself, himself, herself, itself, ourselves, yourselves, themselves* I hurt <u>myself</u>. Sue looked at <u>herself</u> in a mirror.
demonstrative pronouns	These pronouns say that something is nearby (*this, these*) or farther away (*that, those*). <u>These</u> are useful books. <u>Those</u> are useless.

Notice: Demonstrative pronouns stand alone. When one of these words is used in front of a noun, it is usually called a *demonstrative adjective*.

Examples: Give me <u>that</u>. (demonstrative pronoun)
Give me <u>that</u> book. (demonstrative adjective)

Verbs	
transitive verbs	These verbs must be followed by a noun or a word that is used as a noun. If a transitive verb (e.g., *make*) doesn't have a following noun (called a *direct object*; see p. 8), the sentence doesn't make sense. Tom makes mistakes. (good sentence) Tom makes. (strange sentence) Sue thanked me. (good sentence) Sue thanked. (strange sentence)
intransitive verbs	These verbs don't need a following noun. If an intransitive verb (e.g., *sleep*) has a following noun, the sentence doesn't make good sense. Ann sleeps. (good sentence) Ann sleeps her dog. (strange sentence) Ron disappeared. (good sentence) Ron disappeared me. (strange sentence)
auxiliary verbs	These verbs are sometimes called *helping verbs*, and they go before the main verb of a sentence. They are forms of *do*, *have*, and *be*, and they give information about the time (tense) of a verb. (See chapter 2.) The sun <u>does</u> not revolve around the earth. Ron <u>has</u> convinced me to buy a car. Sue <u>is</u> relaxing in front of the TV.

modal auxiliary verbs	These special words go before the main verb and help give it meaning. (See chapter 3.) *can, could, may, might, must, shall, should, will, would* Heavy snow <u>might</u> create a problem at the airport tonight. This room <u>can</u> accommodate thirty students.

Notice: Many verbs can be used both transitively and intransitively.

Examples: Sue <u>walked</u> to school. (intransitive)
Ann <u>walked</u> her dog. (transitive)

Adjectives	
possessive adjectives	These words go in front of nouns and tell who owns something. *my, our, your, his, her, its, their* <u>My</u> cat is nicer than <u>your</u> cat.
articles	These are three special adjectives that go in front of nouns. (See chapter 5.) *The* is called the definite article. *A* and *an* are called indefinite articles.
quantifiers	These are a special kind of adjective that tell the amount (quantity) of a noun. (See chapter 7.) e.g., *all, each, some, any*

There are two additional categories that are also important.

gerunds	These words end in *-ing* and are used as the names of activities. Sometimes they are used alone; sometimes they begin phrases. (See chapter 8.) <u>Skiing</u> is my favorite sport. <u>Walking</u> in the mountains is my favorite way to relax. Sue enjoys <u>receiving</u> letters from home.
infinitives	An infinitive is *to + VERB*. This form of a verb has special uses. (See chapter 8.) Our instructor plans <u>to grade</u> our tests tonight. I hope <u>to get</u> a good grade on the test.

There are many other categories and subcategories of words, but these are the important ones to begin with. Others will be explained as needed in later chapters.

Practice Exercise

Label each word in the following (silly) story.

This is a very sad story. Jim found some magic beans under an enormous pile of dirty laundry in his extremely messy room, but he did not want to keep them. He gave those beans to me, and I put them in a little, tiny box and secretly hid them in my kitchen. Our cat jumped into the cupboard, ate the magic beans, and became a beautiful princess. Unfortunately, this princess cannot speak any human language. She meows and eats mice. I do not like meowing, and she does not like eating mice.

Sentences

Parts of Sentences

A *phrase* is a group of words that works together as a unit. If the main word in a phrase is a noun, the phrase is called a *noun phrase*. If the main word in a phrase is a verb, the phrase is called a *verb phrase*. By the same principle, there are *prepositional phrases, adjective phrases, adverb phrases*, et cetera.

A *clause* is a group of words with both a *subject* and a *predicate*.

Subject	Predicate	
	verb	rest of predicate
I	laughed.	
Birds	fly.	
Big white birds	are eating	juicy worms.
Some fat little birds	are singing	in the trees.
The federal government	has issued	temporary restrictions on air travel.

Notice:
1. A subject is usually a noun phrase or a pronoun.
2. The most important part of a predicate is a verb. Every predicate must have a verb.

Every English sentence contains at least one *independent clause*. An independent clause can stand alone.

A *dependent clause* must be connected to another clause. Dependent clauses almost always begin with a subordinator (e.g., *although, because, that*). (See chapter 10.)

A *simple sentence* has one independent clause.

Examples: We drink coffee.
          Ron and Pat drink tea.

A *compound sentence* has two independent clauses connected by *and, but, or,* or *nor.* Writers usually use a comma between the two clauses, but some writers omit the comma if the clauses are very short.

Examples: We drink coffee, but they drink tea.
          We like coffee, and we like tea.

A *complex sentence* has at least one independent clause and one dependent clause (sometimes more of either kind). Use a comma after the dependent clause if it comes before the independent clause.

Examples: Although we drink coffee, they drink tea.
          We drank coffee while they drank tea.
          We enjoyed the coffee that Kim made.

Practice Exercise

Label the independent and dependent clauses and the subjects and predicates in the following sentences.

1. Pat gave a five-minute speech.

2. Urban areas have a lot of traffic, but rural areas have quiet roads.

3. Although Ann was physically exhausted, she continued working.

4. We appreciate the work that Ann completed.

5. Sue is an intelligent student, but she failed a test because she felt

   emotionally exhausted.

Types of Predicates

Direct Objects

In a predicate with a transitive verb, the noun phrase following the verb is called a *direct object*.

Subject	Predicate		
	verb	**direct object**	rest of predicate
Sue	wrote	her appointment	on the calendar.
Ron	tapes	TV shows	every day on his VCR.
The arrow	hit	the target.	

Indirect Objects

A small group of verbs[3] can have both a direct object and an *indirect object*.

Subject	Predicate			
	verb	**direct object**	**indirect object**	rest of predicate
Pam	gave	gifts	to Ann	last week.
Lee	bought	a calendar	for Tom	at a bookstore.

Subject	Predicate			
	verb	**indirect object**	**direct object**	rest of predicate
Pam	gave	Ann	gifts	last week.
Lee	bought	Tom	a calendar	at a bookstore.

Complements

A small and very important group of verbs link (connect) the subject with an adjective or noun phrase that is called a *complement*.[4] Examples of linking verbs are *be, seem, smell, sound, taste,* and *feel*.

---

3. These verbs are usually called *ditransitive verbs*.

4. Complements are sometimes called *predicate nouns* or *predicate adjectives*.

Subject	Predicate	
	verb	**complement**
This flower	smells	sweet.
Ann	seems	intelligent.
Pat and Jan	are	medical doctors.
UNICEF	is	an international aid organization.

Another small group of verbs takes both a direct object and an *object complement*.

Subject	Predicate		
	verb	**direct object**	**object complement**
Tom	painted	the room	white.
I	consider	Jan	my best friend.

Practice Exercise

Label the subjects, verbs, direct objects, indirect objects, and complements in the following sentences.

1. Civil engineers are inspecting this bridge.

2. This bridge might collapse in an earthquake.

3. The bridge's support columns are weak.

4. The bridge needs reinforcement.

5. The engineers will give the governor their report next week.

6. The engineers are experts on stress in large structures.

Kinds of Sentences

Statements (Also Called *Declarative Sentences*)

In many languages, speakers may leave out a subject or a verb if the meaning of the sentence is easy to understand without them, but in English, there is a very strong rule that statements must have both a subject and a verb.

NOT ENGLISH   Is raining today.
              My father very happy.

ENGLISH   It is raining today.
              My father is very happy.

In some languages, but not in English, the subject may be stated twice, once as a noun and again as a pronoun.

NOT ENGLISH   The dog she bit me.
              A lot of people in this school they like to study
              technical subjects.

ENGLISH   The dog bit me.
              A lot of people in this school like to study technical
              subjects.

English speakers may use two noun phrases to refer to the same person or thing. This structure is called an *appositive*. Notice the use of commas.

Examples: George Washington, the first president of the United States, died
              in 1799.
              Dr. Tan teaches sociology, the study of human social behavior.

Negative Statements

To form a negative statement, place *not* after the first auxiliary or *be*. For all other verb phrases, use *do not (don't), does not (doesn't)* or *did not (didn't)*.

Subject	First Auxiliary or Main Verb *Be*	*Not*	Other Auxiliaries + Main Verb	Rest of Predicate
The school	will	not	impose	a new lab fee.
We	have	not	been paying	a fee to use the lab.
Sue	is	not		low on funds.
Sue	does	not	worry	about money.
Sue	did	not	receive	financial aid for school.

Questions (Also Called *Interrogative Sentences*)

English has several question forms (and they are a little complicated).

Yes-No Questions

To form a yes-no question, move either the first auxiliary verb or *be* forward, before the subject. (This is called *inversion*.) If there is no auxiliary, use *do, does,* or *did.*

First Auxiliary or Main Verb *Be*	Subject	Other Auxiliaries + Main Verb	Rest of Predicate
Will	they	conduct	the experiment?
Have	they	assembled	their equipment?
Are	they	testing	a hypothesis?
Do	they	have	adequate funding for the project?
Did	they	run	preliminary tests on their equipment?

Wh-questions

In questions with *wh*-words *(what, when, where, why, which, whom, whose,* and *how)*, the *wh*-word goes before the moved auxiliary.

Wh-word	First Auxiliary	Subject	Other Auxiliaries + Main Verb	Rest of Predicate
Where	is	Tom	conducting	his research?
How	will	he	evaluate	his data?
What problems	has	he	encountered?	
When	does	he	expect	to finish?
Why	did	he	choose	this topic?

If the *wh*-word is the subject of the question, it stays in subject position.

Subject	Verb Phrase	Rest of Predicate
Who	purchased	this new equipment?
What	will happen	to the old equipment?

Practice Exercises

1. Get acquainted with your classmates. Working with a partner, write a list of 10 questions you can ask other students. Divide into small groups and interview your classmates.
2. Working with a group, play a game of 20 questions. One person in the group thinks of a person, place, or object. Others in the group try to guess what it is. They are allowed to ask up to 20 yes-no questions. If they cannot guess, they lose. If someone guesses, he or she starts the next game. (This game has been popular in the United States for at least two centuries.)

Commands (Also Called *Imperative Sentences*)

Commands are the only sentences in English that don't have a subject.

Examples: Shut the door.
Give me a couple more minutes to finish this assignment, please.
Please don't assign any work to Robert this week.
Have a nice day!

The word *please* softens the tone of a command, but it is still a command. The level of politeness in a command often depends on your tone of voice. Therefore, it is especially important to be careful with written commands (such as in e-mail), where your voice can't be heard. English speakers often use polite requests ("Would you please . . . ," "Could you please . . .") instead of polite commands.

Practice Exercise

With a partner, practice giving each other polite commands (e.g., "Shut the door, please"; "Please give me that book") and making polite requests (e.g., "Would you please shut the door?" "Could you give me that book, please?").

Trouble Spots and Tricky Points

1. In English, the bond between a verb and its direct object is very tight. In many languages, it is possible to put a word between the verb and the object, but in English, if anything comes between a verb and its object, the sentence usually sounds odd.

Good English	Not Good English
Lee deliberately distorted the facts.	Lee distorted deliberately the facts.
Pat coordinated the aid project very well.	Pat coordinated very well the aid project.

2. English has an unusual pattern that is sometimes used to create emphasis in formal speech and writing. In this pattern, a negative phrase is placed at the front of the clause to create an *emphatic form* of the sentence. The subject and verb then invert in the same way that they do in yes-no questions. (The negative words include *only, seldom, hardly,* and *rarely,* as well as *no, not,* and *never.*)

Examples: Never will I deliberately hurt a friend.
Never before in my life have I been so completely abandoned by a friend!
In no way does the mayor's speech contradict her earlier statements.
Only once did we deviate from our plan.

Practice Exercise

Choose a partner. Tell your partner something that you have never done in your life and something that you will never do in your life. Use sentences in emphatic form.

For Discussion and/or Writing

1. What is your "linguistic autobiography"? How did you learn English? Describe the people, places, and experiences that have been important to you in learning English. Were some especially helpful? Why? Were some experiences negative or a waste of time? Why?
2. What are your goals in studying English? What kinds of speaking and writing do you want to do in English someday? What do you want to do in English this year?

3. When you read or write, are you more comfortable using English or another language? What experiences have helped you learn to write (in any language)? What kinds of writing do you feel comfortable doing? What kinds of writing do you dislike doing?
4. What field of study are you interested in? Why is that field of study interesting or important?

Dictionaries

Most people do not own and use enough dictionaries. In fact, most people do not even understand the variety of dictionary types that are available. You can greatly improve your use of a language by using the right dictionary for your needs. Each kind of dictionary has advantages and disadvantages.

Formats

Paperback Dictionaries

Advantages: These dictionaries are lightweight, easy to carry, inexpensive and not difficult to replace if they are lost or damaged.

Disadvantages: These dictionaries don't have room for a large number of words. If a word has eight meanings, a paperback dictionary will probably only give four or five of them. As an advanced student, you often need the less common definitions.

Hardback Dictionaries

Advantages: These dictionaries have room for lots of information, including more words, more definitions of each word, and more usage information.

Disadvantages: They are heavy. No one wants to carry a hardback dictionary everywhere.

Handheld Electronic Dictionaries

Advantages: These dictionaries are wonderfully fast and easy to use.

Disadvantages: These dictionaries are usually expensive, so losing or damaging one is a major loss. They usually contain no more information than a paperback dictionary, although electronic storage capacity is increasing steadily.

CD-ROM Dictionaries

Advantages: These dictionaries have almost unlimited room for information. However, some publishers include a lot of information and others don't. You should evaluate these dictionaries carefully before buying one.

Disadvantage: You must load the dictionary onto a computer and use that computer when you want to use the dictionary, which makes it less portable and less convenient.

Web-Based Dictionaries

Advantages: These dictionaries have almost unlimited room for information if the producer chooses to make use of it. They can be kept up-to-date very easily.

Disadvantage: You must be connected to the Web to use one.

Contents

Bilingual Dictionaries

These dictionaries give translations of English words both from and into another language.

Advantage: If you know how to read another language well, these dictionaries are very easy to understand.

Disadvantages: Because many words do not have exact translations into another language, the translations in these dictionaries are often only approximate. Because these dictionaries must include two languages, there usually isn't room to include a large number of words, much grammar information, or many example sentences.

Summary: Most second language users want to own a bilingual dictionary but need to own other dictionaries too. Bilingual dictionaries are more helpful when you are reading than when you are writing.

Collegiate Dictionaries

These dictionaries are intended to meet the needs of college-educated native speakers and usually have the word *college* or *collegiate* in the title.

Advantages: These dictionaries contain large numbers of English words and include many definitions of each word.

Disadvantages: The definitions are often difficult for a language learner to understand. Also, these dictionaries do not contain very much of the grammar and usage information that second language learners need.

Summary: You will probably want to own a collegiate dictionary, but it should not be your only dictionary.

Learner's Dictionaries

These dictionaries are intended for nonnative speakers of English and range from simple picture dictionaries to very complete dictionaries for advanced users. Because many people all over the world use English as a second language, dictionary companies are competing to develop products that will meet the needs of this large and diverse market. Companies are trying to create dictionaries that you, as a bilingual or second language user, will really like.

Advantages: These dictionaries use fairly simple English, include a lot of information about the grammar and usage of a word, and often include sample sentences, synonyms, and information on word frequency. They also give information on idioms and collocations.

Disadvantage: As your knowledge of English improves, you regularly need to buy a more advanced learner's dictionary.

Summary: These dictionaries are an enormous help to bilingual and second language students.

Specialized Dictionaries

These dictionaries explain the specialized vocabulary of different fields of study. For example, there are dictionaries of music, of economics, and of chemistry. Some are written for college-educated native speakers; others are written for language learners.

Advantages: Everyday words often have very specialized meanings in a particular field of study, but ordinary dictionaries don't give these specialized meanings. Specialized dictionaries do. In addition, specialized dictionaries often give accurate, brief explanations (comprising one to two pages) of basic theories in a field.

Disadvantage: Some of these dictionaries are quite expensive. (The reference section of a school library is often the best place to find and use one.)

Reading a Dictionary Entry

Take time to learn how to read the entries in your dictionary. Each dictionary has its own symbols and abbreviations, and the publisher always includes an explanation of how to read this information.

The example entries printed in this section are from page 930 of the *Longman Advanced American Dictionary* (2000), a learner's dictionary.

> **min·is·try** /ˈmɪnəstri/ *n. plural* **ministries 1 the ministry** the profession of being a church leader, especially in the Protestant church: *Nate felt called to the ministry.* **2** [C] a government department in some countries: *the Ministry of Agriculture* **3** [U] the work done by a priest or other religious person: *Allen has been involved with Lutheran music ministry for more than 20 years.*

In the entry for *ministry,* the symbol [C] denotes a count noun and the symbol [U] denotes a noncount noun. (The *U* comes from the word *uncountable.*)

Practice Exercise

Refer to the dictionary entry for *ministry* to answer the following questions.

1. What does *ministry* mean when it is a count noun? What does *ministry* mean when it is a noncount noun? (For more information on count and noncount nouns, see chapter 5.)
2. What does the phrase *the ministry* mean?

The entries for *minor* on page 18 show that *minor* can be an adjective (adj.), a noun (n.), or a verb (v.). The small divided box in the margin marks high-frequency words, and the numeral 3 shows that *minor* is among the 3,000 most common words of spoken (S) and written (W) English. Some words and a phrase (e.g., MAJOR and MINOR LEAGUES) are printed in all capital letters to indicate that you may also want to look up these terms.

Example entries reprinted by permission of Pearson Education, Inc. White Plains, New York.

s w **mi·nor¹** /ˈmaɪnɚ/ *adj.* **1** small and not very important or serious, especially when compared with other things: *Williams suffered a minor stroke.* | *Most of the problems have been very minor.* | *a minor traffic violation* —opposite MAJOR¹ (1) **2** based on a musical SCALE in which the third note of the related MAJOR scale has been lowered by a half step: *a minor key* | *a symphony in D minor* —compare MAJOR¹ (3)

minor² *n.* [C] **1** LAW someone who is below the age at which they become legally responsible for their actions: *Thomas pleaded guilty to buying alcohol for a minor.* **2** the second main subject that you study in college for your degree: *"What's your minor?" "History."* —compare MAJOR² (2) **3 the minors** the MINOR LEAGUES

minor³ *v.*
  minor in sth *phr. v.* [T] to study a second main subject as part of your college degree: *Nguyen minored in theater studies.* —opposite MAJOR³

Practice Exercise

Refer to the dictionary entries for *minor* to answer the following questions.

1. Some adjectives are used only before nouns. Some adjectives are used only in predicates. Most adjectives are used in both locations. Where can you use *minor?*
2. The noun *minor* has a special meaning in law. What is it?
3. The verb *minor* is used in a particular pattern. The phrase "**minor in** sth" in the dictionary entry means "minor in something." *Minor* is a phrasal verb (phr. v.), and it is transitive (T). Therefore, you can't say, "I am minoring math," or, "I am minoring at college." The sample sentence in the entry shows the correct way to use *minor* as a verb. What is the opposite of the verb *minor?*

For Discussion and/or Writing

1. Which dictionaries do you own? How did you choose them? What do you like and not like about them?
2. What is your favorite English word? Why? Which English word is the most beautiful to you? Which is the ugliest? Why?

Chapter 2
Verb Tenses

Introductory Focus

The word *tense* comes from the Latin word for time. A verb tense tells something about the time of a sentence. Look at the following proverbs and sayings.

Experience is the best teacher.
A stitch in time saves nine.
We have met the enemy, and he is ours.[1]
We have met the enemy, and he is us.[2]
Curiosity killed the cat.
Faint heart never won fair lady.
Eat, drink, and be merry, for tomorrow we die.
Tomorrow is another day.
If you lie down with dogs, you will rise up with fleas.

Do you understand these sayings? Can you think of a time when you might say one of them to a friend? Underline the verb phrases in the sayings. What do you notice about time in these sentences?

The first reference chart in this chapter gives an overall view of English verb tenses,[3] and the charts that follow explain the basic uses of each tense. Native speakers, especially the very good writers, know how to use verb tenses for special (and very subtle) effects. You will sometimes see verbs used in unusual ways, but the rules in this chapter explain most uses of English verbs.

1. Attributed to Lieutenant Oliver Hazard Perry at the battle of Lake Erie in 1813.

2. From the comic strip *Pogo* by Walt Kelly.

3. See also the reference chart titled "The Longest Possible English Verb Phrase" on page 58.

REFERENCE CHART
English Verb Tenses

Column A		Column B	
Past Time Verb Forms		**Present/Future Time Verb Forms**	
Events before basic time (before point in past)	Basic time (point in past)	*Expressing* Events before basic time (before now)	Basic time (now)
↓	↓	↓	↓
Past Perfect I had seen a hawk. They had danced. She had felt happy.	*Simple Past* I saw a hawk. They danced. She felt happy.	*Present Perfect* He has worked all day. She has been kind. I have visited Paris.	*Simple Present* He works at home. You are kind. Paris is in France.
Past Perfect Progressive I had been dancing. We had been eating.	*Past Progressive* I was dancing. We were eating.	*Present Perfect Progressive* I have been eating. He has been sleeping.	*Present Progressive* I am eating a pear. She is sleeping.

Notice:

1. The verb forms in the shaded areas of the chart are not used very frequently, although every native speaker knows them and uses them in certain situations.

2. Linguists say that English doesn't have a true future tense. (There aren't any future tense endings to put on a verb.) There are several ways of indicating future time: using *will*, using *be going to*, and, if an event is scheduled for a specific time, using simple present tense. If you want to create the traditional list of future tenses, take the present tenses, add *will*, and put the following verb in its simple form.

Examples: Simple present → Simple future
Cats chase mice. → *Cats will chase mice.*

Present progressive → Future progressive
Sue is sleeping.   → *Sue will be sleeping.*

Present perfect progressive → Future present progressive
He has been sleeping.   → *He will have been sleeping.*

3. When you write, you should normally choose a basic time—either the past tense group (column A) or the present tense group (column B)—and stay with it. Native speakers do not shift from column to column without a reason. If you shift from one column to the other, you must have a reason, and, usually, you should give a signal to the reader. If you switch columns without a reason, you will confuse the reader, because native language readers will stop and try to figure out your (nonexistent) reason.

Present Tenses

Simple Present Tense

Use	Examples
Statements of principles and general facts	Paris is the capital of France. Water freezes at 0° Celsius.
Current habits and customary actions	I eat cereal for breakfast. Our committee meets on the first Monday of every month.
Stative verbs	The Smiths own a small business. You seem tired.

Notice: Stative verbs almost always use a simple tense instead of a progressive tense. See the list of common stative verbs on page 25.

Present Progressive Tense

be (am, is, are) + present participle *(-ing)*

Use	Examples
Activities and events that are in progress "now" (at the time of speaking or writing)	I am studying English. The committee is drafting a report.

Notice: "Now" can mean "this instant," "this day," "this year," or even "this century," depending on how long a period of time the speaker chooses, but "now" always includes the current moment.

Progressive tenses usually imply that the action may come to an end at some point.

Present Perfect Tense

have or *has* + past participle *(-ed)*

Use	Examples
Events, activities, and states "before now," "before the basic time of my story"	I have visited Paris three times. Ann has never been unkind to me. Water has eroded the banks of this river.
Activities and states that began "before now" and continue up to "now"	I have lived in Seattle for twelve years. (I still live in Seattle.) Sue has studied for three hours without a break. (She is still studying.)
With time phrases (such as *since*) that tell when the time "before now" began	We have lived here since 1987. I have not smoked since January.

Notice:

1. The present perfect tense is a present time verb tense and is never used with a reference to a specific time in the past.
2. In sentences with *since,* the main clause uses a perfect tense. Other phrases that are used to express the length of the period of time "before now" include the following:

    For the past hour (or few days, week, month, year, etc.), . . .
    During the past few days (or weeks, months, years, etc.), . . .

3. Most students find it hard to see a difference between "before now" and "past." The difference is not in when the event happened but in the basic time frame the speaker or writer is using. Present perfect tenses are part of telling a story in present time. The speaker tells a story in the basic time frame of "now" and uses the present perfect tense to express events "before now." If the speaker or writer switches to a specific time in the past, he or she switches to past tense (and should give a signal).

    Example: I like to travel, and I want to go to Europe this summer. Although I have never been to Spain, I have visited France twice. My parents took me there when I was five years old, and I visited Paris again last year.

4. The present perfect tense is not normally used with actions by dead people because dead people aren't part of life "now."

    Example: Thomas Edison invented the lightbulb. (Not: Thomas Edison has invented the lightbulb.)

Present Perfect Progressive Tense

have/has + *been* + present participle *(-ing)*

Use	Examples
Activities that began in the past and continue up to the present	Would you like to go get coffee with me? I have been studying for three hours, and I really need a break. Tom, I'd like you to meet Pam. She has been designing a new Web page that I think will be very helpful to us.

Notice:

1. The present perfect progressive tense isn't needed very often.
2. It is usually used in conversations rather than in writing.
3. It is usually used only once or perhaps twice at the beginning of a conversation to explain the current situation to a newcomer.[4]

Practice Exercise

Complete each of the following sentences with the present perfect form of the verb in parentheses. Refer to the irregular verb chart beginning on page 29 if necessary.

a. Ana _____ (complete) her research project on frogs.

b. She _____ (write) a 30-page paper.

c. Several students _____ (not, finished) their projects yet.

d. The instructor _____ (extend) the deadline for completing the projects.

e. The projects _____ (take) more time than was expected.

---

4. This information comes from a presentation by M. Celce-Murcia and N. Yoshida, "Understanding and Teaching the Present Perfect Progressive," at the 1998 TESOL convention.

Practice Exercises

1. Write a list of five or six facts about your habits, likes, and dislikes. Share them with a partner or small group.
2. Choose a famous person. What is he or she probably doing right now? Write five sentences. (Classes may want to write celebrities' names on slips of paper and let each person take a name.)
3. Make a list of five strange things you have done or have never done. Four sentences should be true, and one should be a lie. Working with a partner or small group, read the sentences. Try to guess which sentences are false.

1. Think of a commercial service that you use (perhaps a long-distance phone company, an Internet service provider, a school meal plan, or a favorite restaurant). How long have you used this company? How well do you like it? What are the pluses and minuses of this company's services?
2. What are you trying to accomplish this week? What have you already accomplished?

Future

English does not have a true future tense, but there are several ways to indicate future time.

Ways to Indicate Future Time	Examples
will	The primary theme of the president's speech will be peace. The speech will begin at 8:00 tomorrow. I will help you work for peace.
be going to	The second theme of the speech is going to be prosperity. The speech is going to begin at 8:00 tomorrow. We are going to listen to the president's speech.
simple present tense	The speech begins at 8:00 tomorrow.

Notice:
1. Speakers use both *will* and *be going to* to make predictions about the future.
2. Speakers usually use *will* when they make a promise or volunteer to do something.
3. Speakers use *be going to* for future plans (events and actions).
4. If an event is scheduled for a specific time, speakers often use simple present tense.

English does not use *will* in dependent clauses with time words (*after, before, when,* etc.).

NOT ENGLISH	We will watch TV after Ron will get home tonight.
	Ron will eat before he will watch his favorite comedy series.
	When a drama will come on, Ron will change to another channel.
ENGLISH	We will watch TV after Ron gets home tonight.
	Ron will eat before he watches his favorite comedy series.
	When a drama comes on, Ron will change to another channel.

For Discussion and/or Writing

1. What are your plans for the coming weekend?
2. What will you do after you finish school?

Common Stative Verbs

The following verbs are not usually used in progressive tenses.

hear	be	know	need	own	include
smell	seem	believe	want	belong	contain
taste	appear	understand	prefer	have	comprise
see	look	think	like		consist
feel		suppose	love		
		mean			

Exceptions:
1. *See,* unless you mean "visiting," as in "He's seeing a doctor every week for his allergies."
2. *Look,* unless you mean "searching," as in "I'm looking for my pen."
3. *Think,* unless you mean that your brain is processing an idea right now, as in "I'm thinking about my mother's chocolate cake."
4. *Have,* unless you mean "organizing, planning," as in "We're having a party next week."

Notice: The English language is slowly changing over the years. Current English speakers use progressive tenses more often than they did a hundred years ago, and you may occasionally hear these stative verbs used with progressive tenses.

Practice Exercises

1. Write five sentences about your needs, wants, and preferences.
2. At this moment, what do you hear, smell, see, and feel?
3. Choose a partner and write sentences about him/her. Use *be*, *seem*, *appear*, and *look*.

Past Tenses

Simple Past Tense

Past participle (*-ed* or an irregular verb form). See the chart of irregular verb forms at the end of this chapter.

Use	Examples
Events in the past	We bought a car yesterday. Thomas Edison developed the first lightbulb.

Notice:
1. The simple past indicates that events are not imaginary; they happened at some specific past time.[5]
2. General principles are usually stated in the present tense; examples which show that the principles are true are usually stated in the past tense.

   Example: Earthquakes are sometimes enormously destructive. In August 1999, an earthquake injured over 50,000 people in Turkey, and in January 2001, an earthquake injured more than 160,000 people in India.

Past Progressive Tense: *Was/Were* + Present Participle (*-ing*)

Use	Examples
Actions in progress at some point in the past	We were eating dinner when the phone rang. Balboa was looking for riches in Central America when he became the first European to see the Pacific Ocean. Ann was watching TV while Sue was cleaning the house.

5. Of course, fiction and other imaginative work may be told in the past tense. An honest author lets the reader know that the writing is fiction.

Notice:

1. The past progressive tense is usually used to indicate that one action was in progress when another action occurred.
2. The past progressive tense is sometimes used to indicate that two activities were in progress at the same time.

Past Perfect Tense: *Had* + **Past Participle** *(-ed)*

Use	Examples
Actions previous to the time of a past event	We had already eaten dinner when Tom arrived. He wanted to eat, so we gave him leftovers. Balboa fled to Central America because he had gone deeply into debt in Hispaniola.

Notice:

1. The past perfect tense shows that an event occurred "before the basic time of my story." In the first of the preceding examples, the basic story begins at the time that Tom arrived. In the second example, the author will continue talking about Balboa's life in Central America, not his life in Hispaniola.
2. Do not overuse the past perfect tense. Native speakers do not use the past perfect tense very often. If the context makes the time relationship clear, they use the simple past, not the past perfect.

> *Examples:* Tom arrived after we finished dinner.
> Balboa went deeply into debt before he left Hispaniola.

Past Perfect Progressive Tense: *Had* + *Been* + **Present Participle** *(-ing)*

Use	Examples
Activities in progress before and continuing up to a past event.	We had been studying for three hours when the fire alarm rang. The company had been losing money every year until Sam Lee took charge of the corporate finances in 2002.

Notice: This tense is not needed very often, but every native speaker knows it and can use it.

Practice Exercise

Fill in each blank with an appropriate form of the verb in parentheses.

In 1891, James Naismith _____ (invent) the game of basketball. Naismith _____ (teach) physical education at the School for Christian Workers in Springfield, Massachusetts, and bored students in the school _____ (need) a new indoor sport. Although Naismith _____ (spend) most of his life teaching physical education, by the end of his life, he _____ _____ (earn) degrees in the fields of philosophy, religion, physical education, and medicine.

Today, basketball _____ (become) an international sport. More than 300 million people around the world _____ (play) basketball. Each year, players from many countries _____ (compete) for positions on professional teams in the U.S. Basketball first _____ _____ (become) an Olympic sport in 1936, and since then, teams from many countries _____ (play) against each other in international competitions.

Practice Exercises

1. Make a list of the five most important things you did last year.
2. Interview five classmates. Ask them, "What were you doing at 5:15 P.M. yesterday?"

For Discussion and/or Writing

1. Think of a time in your childhood when you or your friends did something funny, disobedient, or dangerous. What happened?
2. What kind of classroom atmosphere do you think is most helpful for learning a language? State your general answer in the present tense and then use examples from your experience or the experience of others to support your answer.
3. Pick an event from the past 10 years that has had an impact on your family, community, or nation. What happened? When? What were the initial effects? How has this event continued to affect lives? What are the current effects? Can you make a prediction about its effects in the future? (You should give a signal when you change from past time to present time. Some good signals are *now, currently, more recently, today,* and *since then.*)
4. Describe the life of some living person that you know or know about. (A family member is a good choice. You might also choose a famous person that you admire or someone who has influenced you as a role model.) What was this person's life like in the past? What did he or she do? What is this person's life like now? What is he or she doing?
5. Our tastes often change over the years. How have your opinions about music (or clothing styles) changed? What did you like when you were younger? What do you like now?
6. Describe a time when you rejected advice from your parents or close friends. Do you now think that you made the right choice? Why or why not?

REFERENCE CHART
150 Irregular Verbs

The overall tendency is for verbs to become regular. This is an ongoing process, so some verbs (such as *kneel*) have both a regular and an irregular form. You may occasionally hear an irregular form for verbs that are not listed here (such as *learn, learnt, learnt*), and you may hear one of these verbs used as a regular verb (such as *broadcast, broadcasted*).

Verb	Simple Past	Past Participle
arise	arose	arisen
be	was/were	been
bear	bore	borne/born
beat	beat	beaten
become	became	become
begin	began	begun
bend	bent	bent
bet	bet	bet
bid	bade/bid	bidden
bind	bound	bound
bite	bit	bitten
bleed	bled	bled
blow	blew	blown
break	broke	broken
breed	bred	bred
bring	brought	brought
broadcast	broadcast	broadcast
build	built	built
burst	burst	burst
buy	bought	bought
cast	cast	cast
catch	caught	caught
choose	chose	chosen
cling	clung	clung
come	came	come
cost	cost	cost

Verb	Simple Past	Past Participle
creep	crept	crept
cut	cut	cut
deal	dealt	dealt
dig	dug	dug
do	did	done
draw	drew	drawn
drink	drank	drunk
drive	drove	driven
eat	ate	eaten
fall	fell	fallen
feed	fed	fed
feel	felt	felt
fight	fought	fought
find	found	found
flee	fled	fled
fling	flung	flung
fly	flew	flown
forbid	forbade/forbad	forbidden
forecast	forecast	forecast
forget	forgot	forgotten
forgive	forgave	forgiven
forgo	forwent	forgone
forsake	forsook	forsaken
freeze	froze	frozen
get	got	got/gotten
give	gave	given

Verb	Simple Past	Past Participle
go	went	gone
grind	ground	ground
grow	grew	grown
hang	hung[6]	hung
have	had	had
hear	heard	heard
hide	hid	hidden
hit	hit	hit
hold	held	held
hurt	hurt	hurt
keep	kept	kept
kneel	knelt/kneeled	knelt/kneeled
knit	knit/knitted	knit/knitted
know	knew	known
lay	laid	laid
lead	led	led
leave	left	left
lend	lent	lent
let	let	let
lie	lay	lain
light	lit/lighted	lit/lighted
lose	lost	lost
make	made	made
mean	meant	meant

---

6. When *hang* means "execute a person by hanging," it is a regular verb, with the past form *hanged*.

Verb	Simple Past	Past Participle
meet	met	met
mislay	mislaid	mislaid
mistake	mistook	mistaken
offset	offset	offset
pay	paid	paid
put	put	put
quit	quit	quit
read	read	read
rid	rid/ridded	rid/ridded
ride	rode	ridden
ring	rang	rung
rise	rose	risen
run	ran	run
say	said	said
see	saw	seen
seek	sought	sought
sell	sold	sold
send	sent	sent
set	set	set
shake	shook	shaken
shed	shed	shed
shine	shone	shone
shoot	shot	shot
show	showed	shown/showed
shrink	shrank/shrunk	shrunk/shrunken
shut	shut	shut

Verb	Simple Past	Past Participle
sing	sang	sung
sink	sank/sunk	sunk
sit	sat	sat
sleep	slept	slept
slide	slid	slid
slit	slit	slit
speak	spoke	spoken
speed	sped	sped
spend	spent	spent
spin	spun	spun
spit	spit/spat	spit/spat
spread	spread	spread
spring	sprang/sprung	sprung
stand	stood	stood
steal	stole	stolen
stick	stuck	stuck
sting	stung	stung
stink	stank/stunk	stunk
strike	struck	struck
strive	strove	striven
swear	swore	sworn
sweep	swept	swept
swim	swam	swum
swing	swung	swung
take	took	taken
teach	taught	taught

Verb	Simple Past	Past Participle
tear	tore	torn
tell	told	told
think	thought	thought
throw	threw	thrown
thrust	thrust	thrust
tread	trod	trodden/trod
undergo	underwent	undergone
underlie	underlay	underlain
understand	understood	understood
undertake	undertook	undertaken
upset	upset	upset
wake	woke/waked	woken/waked
wear	wore	worn
weave	wove	woven
wed	wed/wedded	wed/wedded
weep	wept	wept
win	won	won
wind	wound	wound
withdraw	withdrew	withdrawn
withstand	withstood	withstood
write	wrote	written
wring	wrung	wrung

Chapter 3
Modals

Introductory Focus

The words *can, could, may, might, must, shall, should, will,* and *would* are called *modals* or *modal auxiliaries.* Semimodals[1] are very short phrases which are used like modals: *be going to, be supposed to, had better, have to, have got to, ought to,* and *used to.* As an advanced learner of English, you probably already use many of the modals well. This chapter will give you opportunities to review modals you know and to practice some of the tricky points that cause trouble for most English learners. The following proverbs and sayings use modals.

You can lead a horse to water, but you can't make it drink.
Two can keep a secret, if one of them is dead.
Money can't buy happiness.
You have to learn to walk before you can run.
All good things must come to an end.
You should not confuse your career with your life.

Have you heard any of these sayings? What do they mean? Do you agree with them? Underline the modal in each saying. What does the modal mean?

Background Information

The modals are a very useful group of words. A speaker uses a modal to quickly change the meaning of a sentence, as in the following examples.

---

1. In some books, these are called *marginal auxiliaries, quasi-modals,* or *periphrastic modals.*

I speak Spanish.
I can speak Spanish. (I am able to speak Spanish.)
I might speak Spanish. (Maybe I will speak Spanish sometime.)
I must speak Spanish. (It is necessary for me to speak Spanish.)
I should speak Spanish. (The right thing for me to do is to speak
Spanish.)

Unfortunately, although modals are useful, they are also hard to
define because most of them have more than one meaning and must
be understood in context. For example, *may* and *might* are sometimes
synonyms and mean that something is possible but not sure.

Examples: It might rain tonight.
It may rain tonight.

In addition, *may* and *can* are sometimes synonyms and mean that
something is permitted.

Examples: You may smoke in the lounge.
You can smoke in the lounge.

However, although *may* and *might* are sometimes synonyms and
although *may* and *can* are sometimes synonyms, *might* and *can* are
never synonyms.

The meanings and uses of modals have been slowly changing
throughout the history of English. For example, in the past, speakers
frequently used *shall* for future time. Now, *shall* is a rare word. In the
recent past, children were taught to use only *may* for permission.
Now, people more often use *can* for permission. When the style of
a sentence is a little old-fashioned, a well-read English speaker
recognizes that and expects a slightly old-fashioned use of a modal.
As you read more and more types of English writing, you will
become comfortable with unusual uses of modals. The charts in
this chapter describe the way most American English speakers use
modals today.

Modals and Their Meanings

As you review the modals in the following charts, notice that a verb
after a modal is always in its very simple form and never ends in *-s,
-ed,* or *-ing.*

Time

Modals can be used to indicate the time when a situation or action occurred.

Future Time	Past Time
will, shall (rare), *be going to* Boston will levy a new tax on hotels. We are going to visit Boston.	*used to* (situations and repeated actions), *would* (repeated actions) We used to live in New York. We would go to Central Park every week. We would often walk in Central Park.

Notice:

1. *Used to* implies that a situation or action no longer happens.
2. If you ever need a past form of *will* (in reported speech, for example), use *would*.
3. When talking about repeated past actions, speakers often begin with *used to* in the first sentence and continue the story using *would*.

> *Example:* Elementary schools in the United States used to place a lot of emphasis on memorization because memorizing was considered good mental exercise. As part of their geography lessons, teachers would require students to memorize the capital cities of all the states in the United States. In arithmetic, students would memorize the multiplication tables. In history lessons, students would memorize long lists of dates.

For Discussion and/or Writing

Describe what you usually did on Sundays when you were a child. In your description, practice using *used to* and *would*. If Sunday was a regular school day for you, choose another (free) day of the week.

Ability

Modals can be used to express what someone or something is capable of doing or becoming.

Present/Future Time	Past Time
can Some bacteria can survive at extremely high temperatures. Research can be very time consuming.	*could* (not used for one-time events) Sue could speak three languages by the time she was twelve.

Present/Future Time Negative	Past Time Negative
can not, cannot, can't We cannot guarantee this product. I can't find my keys.	*could not, couldn't* I could not find my keys yesterday. Sue couldn't ride a bike when she was young.

Notice:

1. *Cannot* is the traditional spelling. *Can not* is growing in popularity.
2. Don't use *could* for things that happened at one specific time in the past. Instead, use *was/were able to*. If you say, "I could meet with my professor," the listener will think you are talking about a future possibility. If you say, "I could meet with my professor yesterday," the listener will become confused. It is better to say, "I was able to meet with my professor yesterday."

Practice Exercise

Correct the errors in the following sentences.

a. We can assured you that the report will be ready on Friday.

b. I could finish writing my essay for English last night.

c. I don't can focus my mind on my work today.

d. This species of tree can to tolerate dry summers.

For Discussion and/or Writing

1. Identify special abilities you have, abilities you do not have, and abilities you had when you were very young. Use *can* and *could*. Use the following list for ideas, but use your own ideas too.

make friends easily	survive in a wilderness	understand mathematics
whistle	win debates	sew
tell jokes	write poetry	draw cartoons
create Web pages	find bargains	cook something delicious

2. Think of three skills that you can teach to others. Describe them. How did you learn these skills? If there is time available, arrange an opportunity to teach a skill to the class.

Necessity

Modals can be used to express that something is required or necessary, not optional.

Present/Future Time	Past Time
must, must not (indicates something is prohibited), *have to, have got to* (informal) Airlines must enforce the law. Passengers must not take a weapon on an airplane. I have to cancel my appointment with the dentist this afternoon. I've got to study tonight.	*had to* I had to take a test yesterday. We had to condense our report to three pages. They had to submit their research proposal to a committee for approval.

Present/Future Time Negative	Past Time Negative
do not have to (It isn't required or necessary.) Tom doesn't have to take any more English classes. We don't have to leave until 4:00. You don't have to rewrite this paper unless you want to.	*did not have to* (It wasn't required or necessary.) Sue didn't have to take biology in high school. We didn't have to make any drastic cuts in our budget.

Notice:

1. *Must* with this meaning is a strong word and is usually used in official announcements or by people in authority. If you use *must* quite frequently, people may think you have an unpleasant personality.
2. There is a big difference between *must not* (something is prohibited) and *do not have to* (something is not required).
3. In conversation, *have to* is often pronounced "hafta," and *got to* is often pronounced "gotta." In writing, be sure to use the correct spellings.

Practice Exercise

Correct the errors in the following sentences.

a. Sue has better cancel her appointment.

b. Smoking should not being allowed near hospitals.

c. Tom should obtained a schedule of classes before he tried to register for
   next semester.

d. We must to consult an attorney before we sign this contract.

e. Passengers don't have to take a bomb on an airplane.

For Discussion and/or Writing

Tell in detail what you have to do this week and what you had to do last
week. Use *must, have to, have got to, do not have to, had to, did not have to.*

Advisability and Hindsight

Modals can be used to express that an action is good, right, wise, or
appropriate.

Present/Future Time	Past Time
should, ought to, had better (strong, informal), *better* (strong, very informal) Parents should take good care of their children. Tom ought to consult an attorney. Sue had better see a doctor about her cough.	*should have, ought to have, had better have* (strong, informal) Sue should have conferred with an attorney. They ought to have appealed the court's decision. Tom had better have taken good care of the stereo that he borrowed from me!

Present/Future Time Negative	Past Time Negative
should not, ought not (rare), *had better not* (strong, informal), *better not* (strong, very informal) You shouldn't ignore your friends. I ought not forget this appointment. You'd better not try to steal my book!	*should not have, ought not to have* (less common), *better not have* (strong, very informal) Tom should not have spent $300 on a pair of shoes. He shouldn't have thrown away his receipt. Tom's brother better not have thrown the $300 shoes into the trash!

Notice:

1. The past time forms are used to express hindsight. The speaker is looking back at the past and giving advice about the past (too late) or explaining that some action was unwise.
2. The forms with *had better* or *better* are informal and are not used in academic writing. They are strong, warn of possible negative consequences, and are sometimes used in threats.
3. *Ought to* is often pronounced "oughta." *Should have* is often pronounced "shoulda" or "should of." In writing, be sure to use the correct spellings.

Expectation

Modals can be used to express that something is expected, likely, or follows correct guidelines.

Present/Future Time	Past Time
be supposed to It's supposed to rain tomorrow. The parking permit in the car is supposed to be clearly visible at all times. Members of the tennis team are supposed to practice every day.	*was/were supposed to* (implies the action didn't happen) The committee was supposed to present its preliminary report yesterday.

Present/Future Time Negative	Past Time Negative
be not supposed to (indicates something is unexpected or not in obedience to guidelines) It isn't supposed to snow here in May. We are not supposed to chew gum in class.	*was/were not supposed to* They weren't supposed to complete their final report until next Friday, but they finished it early.

Notice:

1. These expressions often suggest a small lack of certainty.
2. *Should* and *be supposed to* often overlap. In many cases, there is little difference between expectation and advisability. In other cases, there is little difference between expectation and logical predictability.
3. Like the other semimodals, *be supposed to* is more frequent in conversation than in academic writing.

Practice Exercise

Correct the errors in the following sentences.

a. Sue should of repeated the laboratory experiments.

b. She knows she not supposed to use that old data for her report.

c. We're not suppose to leave the lab unlocked.

d. We had better checked the locks twice.

e. We should to report to the police any suspicious activities near the lab.

For Discussion and/or Writing

What are the family roles and expectations in your community? How should parents treat their children? How should siblings treat each other? How should married adults treat their in-laws? How should children show respect for their parents? Try to use *should, shouldn't, must, ought to,* et cetera, in your answers.

Options

Modals can be used to indicate that something is an available choice, option, or possibility.

Present/Future Time	Past Time
could	*could have*
We could go to a movie tonight. Where is Tom? Well, he could be in the library or he could be in the computer lab.	I don't know where Sue went last night, but she could have gone to the movies or she could have gone to a concert. I could have gone to Harvard (but I went to the University of Washington instead).

Notice: When used in the first person (with *I* or *we*), *could have* implies that the action did not happen.

Practice Exercises

1. Working with a partner or small group, make a list of things you could do to have fun next weekend.
2. Write five sentences about things you could have done last week but didn't do.

For Discussion and/or Writing

Choose an ordinary household object, such as a hammer, a pencil, or a piece of string. Describe some of the unusual ways in which you could use the object.

Certainty and Lack of Certainty

Speakers also use the modals and semimodals to express how certain they are of a statement. This use of the modals varies a little in different kinds of English. The following chart explains how most Americans use modals to express certainty.

Level of Certainty	Present/Future Time	Past Time
Very logically predictable (The speaker is about 95% sure.)	*must* They left for the airport two hours ago. They must be there by now. *must not* (never *mustn't*) Tom never eats chocolate. He must not like it.	*must have* The ground is wet. It must have rained last night. *must not have* Sue didn't finish her meal. She must not have been hungry.
Fairly logically predictable (The speaker is perhaps 80% sure.)	*should* They left for the airport one hour ago. They should be there by now. *should not* He has worked for only 20 minutes. He shouldn't be tired.	*should have* If they started working last Monday, they should have finished by last Wednesday. *should not have* Driving in the snow yesterday shouldn't have been a problem for Sue. Her car had snow tires.

Level of Certainty	Present/Future Time	Past Time
Possible (The speaker is perhaps less than 50% sure.)	*might, may* Sue might/may know the answer to this question. *might not* (never *mightn't*), *may not* (never *mayn't*) She might not/may not pass her English class this term.	*might have/may have* Sue can't find her keys. She may have/might have locked them inside her car. *might not have/may not have* Tom didn't do well on the test. He might not have/may not have studied.
Not impossible (There is at least a small chance.)	*could* It could snow tonight.	*could have* We're not sure what caused the fire. There could have been an electrical problem.
Impossible (The speaker is 99% sure it isn't true. These modals are often used with emphatic tone.)	*couldn't* Tom couldn't be from France; he doesn't speak any French. *can't* Sue can't be 60 years old; she looks 30.	*couldn't have* He couldn't have arrived before I did. I was the first person to get there. *can't possibly have* She can't possibly have borrowed Tom's car because I had the only key to it in my pocket.

Practice Exercise

Study this information from *The United States Statistical Abstract* and try to imagine how these accidents happened.[2] Create sentences telling what might have happened, could have happened, can't possibly have happened, et cetera. Then create sentences of advice on how people can avoid these accidents.

Examples: The injured people might have dropped trash baskets on their feet.
These people must have cut themselves with their saws.
You should never use a lawn mower while you are barefoot.

---

2. This exercise was inspired by a hilarious essay in *I'm a Stranger Here Myself: Notes on Returning to America after Twenty Years Away,* by Bill Bryson (New York: Broadway Books, 1999).

Injuries Associated with Consumer Products

(These are estimates of the number of people who entered hospital emergency rooms during one year because of accidents with these products.)

Saws (hand or power)	79,854	Windows	131,333
Hammers	41,518	Glass doors	33,952
Knives	435,275	Televisions	37,401
Tableware and flatware	107,963	Footwear	75,804
Waste containers, trash baskets, etc.	26,686	Hair grooming equipment	24,974
Beds	394,939	Jewelry	54,720
Chairs	260,055	Razors and shavers	40,773
Toilets	44,335	Lawn mowers	60,804
Sinks	20,420	Bicycles	544,561
Ceilings and walls	238,066	Skateboards	48,186

Trouble Spots and Tricky Points

1. *may* and *maybe*

May be (modal + VERB) sounds just like the adverb *maybe*. Be careful not to confuse them. In the following sentences, *may* and *be* are separate words.

> Sue may be sick today.
> The newspaper report may be in error.
> Pat may be going to buy a car next week.

The adverb *maybe* is similar in meaning to *perhaps*. It is usually (but not always) used at the beginning of a clause.

Examples: Maybe Sue is sick today.
  Maybe the newspaper report was in error.
  I think maybe I will major in astronomy.
  We are going to have a party, maybe.

Practice Exercises

1. Correct the errors in the following sentences.

   a. Mary maybe going to attend a conference next month.

   b. Maybe Tom happy to assist with her preparations for the conference.

   c. May be the conference delegates will discuss emerging trends in education.

   d. Some trends may be obvious, but others maybe subtle.

2. Complete each of the following sentences with *maybe* or *may be*.

   a. Tom _____ in the lab right now.

   b. _____ he will accomplish a lot today.

   c. He _____ working with acids.

   d. Tom thinks _____ he will finish his project soon.

---

2. *must* and *must have*

Must is used in present/future time and has two possible meanings. *Must have* is used in past time and has only one meaning.

The first meaning of *must* is necessity.

Example: I must pay my rent tomorrow.

The second meaning of *must* is strong certainty.

Example: The baby is crying. She must be hungry.

Must have has only one meaning: great certainty about a past event.

Example: The ground is wet this morning. It must have rained last night.

If you want to say that something was necessary in the past, use *had to*.

Example: I had to pay my rent yesterday.

Practice Exercise

Complete each of the following sentences with *must, must have, have to,* or *had to* and a correct form of the verb in parentheses.

a. Bliss Jewelry _____ (cater) to an upscale clientele. Most of their products are quite expensive.

b. Jim Taylor bought a $10,000 watch at Bliss Jewelry last week. He

_____ (buy) it as a status symbol.

c. When he bought the watch, Jim _____ (pay) an additional $800 in sales tax on it.

d. Now Jim _____ (be) very careful not to wear his watch in public places where there may be pickpockets.

e. Jim _____ (think) that wearing an expensive watch will enhance his image.

---

3. *could* and *could have*

The words *could* and *could have* are a little tricky because *could* is used both in present/future time and in past time. *Could have* is used only in past time.

Present/Future Time
In present/future time, *could* says that something is possible or is an option.

If you want to say that something is not possible, use *can't* or *couldn't*. If you want to say that something is not an option, use *can't*.

Examples: It could snow tonight and that tree could fall over in the storm. (possible)
It can't snow tonight because the temperature is far too warm. (impossible)
A small child couldn't climb this tree. (impossible)
I could go to a movie tonight or I could stay home and watch TV. (options)
We can't go out to a movie tonight, but we could stay home and watch a movie on TV. (not an option/option)

Past Time

In past time, *could* expresses a general ability.

If you want to say that someone did not have an ability, use *couldn't* or *wasn't able to.*

Example: When she entered the university last year, Sue could read Latin and program computers, but she couldn't drive a car and she wasn't able to speak French.

Could have says that something was possible or was an available option.

If you want to say that something was not possible or not an option, use *couldn't have.*

Examples: I could have gotten an A on that test.
We could have studied harder.
Sue couldn't have stolen the computer. She was at my house when the theft occurred.

Practice Exercise

Complete each of the following sentences with *could, couldn't, could have,* or *couldn't have* and an appropriate form of the verb in parentheses.

a. Our project needs greater funding. We _____ (ask) for more money.

b. More money _____ (solve) a lot of problems.

c. Last year, we _____ (predict) the need for a bigger budget.

d. The budget committee worked very, very hard. They _____ (work) harder.

e. Last year's committee members were very skilled. All of them

_____ (use) computer-based accounting programs.

Polite Forms

Many of the modals are used in polite requests and suggestions. These phrases usually need to be understood in context, and the degree of politeness often depends on the tone of voice. Adding the word *please* is a way to increase the level of politeness.

Suggestions	Examples
Why don't we . . . ?	Why don't we quit work now?
Why don't you . . . ?	Why don't you rest for a few minutes?
Shall we . . . ?	Shall we end the meeting now?
Shall I . . . ?	Shall I call Ron and invite him to the party?
Would you like to . . . ?	Would you like to go to a movie with me?
You/We/I could . . .	You could rent a TV instead of buying one.
	We could go to a movie tonight.
	I could meet you at 2:00 if you are free then.

Notice:
1. The phrase *shall I* both makes a suggestion and asks for permission to do something.
2. The phrase *would you like to* is also used for invitations.
3. *Could* makes a suggestion by reminding the listener of an option.

Requests for Permission	Examples
May I/we . . . ?	May I borrow your pen?
Can I/we . . . ?	Can I use your pen for a minute?
Could I/we . . . ?	Could we please borrow your car?
Would you mind if I/we . . . ?	Would you mind if I borrowed your car tomorrow?
	Would you mind if we opened the windows?

Notice:
1. Some people don't like to use *can* for permission, but most Americans use *can* more often than *may* when they ask permission. *May* is a little more formal.
2. *Would you mind if* is followed by a past tense verb form, but it refers to a present or future event. The reply "No, I don't mind" gives permission.

Requests for Action by Others	Examples
Would you . . . ?	Would you please come here for a minute?
Could you . . . ?	Could you open the window for us?
Will you . . . ?	Will you please turn off the radio?
Can you . . . ?	Can you lend me $10?
Would you mind . . . ?	Would you mind turning off the radio?

Notice:

1. *Would* and *could* are a little more formal and polite than *will* and *can*.
2. The polite way to reply to *would you mind* is "No, I wouldn't mind at all."

Practice Exercise

Working with a partner or small group, write a script for a short role play about some extremely polite people. Either choose one of the following situations or create a situation of your own.

> The extremely polite people want to go out to dinner and need to choose a restaurant.
> The extremely polite people are preparing to give a group oral report.
> The extremely polite people are arranging a car pool.
> The extremely polite people are deciding how to take turns using one computer.

For Discussion and/or Writing

1. Imagine that you have been invited to speak to a group of new immigrant parents who want your advice about raising children in a country with a culture that is new to them. What should parents know about the challenges their children will face? What can parents do to make adjusting to a new culture easier for their children?
2. Imagine that you have been invited to speak to a group of students who are preparing to enter school in another country. What can they do to prepare for this experience? What should they remember to take with them? What problems should they expect to face as they adjust to their new situation?
3. Choose a country. Imagine that you have been invited to speak to a group of new residents in that country (business representatives, students, or embassy staff, perhaps). What should they do to experience the best of that country? What must they do to fit in well in that country?
4. Discuss ways in which you think individuals can help themselves cope with psychological stress. What should a person do if stress in his or her life becomes too intense?

Chapter 4
Passive Voice

Introductory Focus

In ordinary use, the adjective *passive* describes someone or something that is not actively involved in a situation. A passive person "just sits there and lets things happen." In grammar, *passive* is the name for certain verb forms. If a sentence is in *passive voice,* the subject of the sentence doesn't *do* the action of the verb; instead, the subject *receives* the action of the verb. The following sayings contain passive verb forms.

> It's no use to lock the barn after the horse has been stolen.
> A tree is known by its fruit.
> The road to hell is paved with good intentions.
> All men are created equal and are endowed by their creator with certain unalienable rights.

Do you understand these sentences? Do you agree with them? Underline the subjects and the verb phrases. Does the subject perform an action?

Forming Passive Voice Verb Phrases

Passive verb phrases use *be* plus the past participle of the main verb.

Passive sentences often (but not always) have equivalent active sentences. The subject of a passive sentence is the direct object of the equivalent active sentence. Passive sentences sometimes use phrases that begin with *by* to express the subject of the active sentence.

Active Sentence	Passive Sentence
Someone completed the first phase of the project.	The first phase of the project was completed.
Someone used inferior materials.	Inferior materials were used.
The governor's staff prepared a report on the problem.	A report on the problem was prepared by the governor's staff.
Further investigation confirmed the report.	The report was confirmed by further investigation.

Tense	Active Voice	Passive Voice
simple present	I label the disks.	The disks are labeled.
present progressive	We are labeling the disks.	The disks are being labeled.
present perfect	She has labeled the disks.	The disks have been labeled.
present perfect progressive	They have been labeling the disks.	The disks have been being labeled.
simple past	We accomplished a lot.	A lot was accomplished.
past progressive	They were accomplishing a lot.	A lot was being accomplished.
past perfect	He had accomplished a lot.	A lot had been accomplished.
past perfect progressive	I had been accomplishing a lot.	A lot had been being accomplished.

Notice: All these passive voice tenses exist, but people rarely use the progressive ones.

Modal verb phrases can also be passive, as in the following examples.

Active Sentence	Passive Sentence
People should maximize profits.	Profits should be maximized.
People should have maximized profits.	Profits should have been maximized.
The ads will not promote smoking.	Smoking will not be promoted.
Someone must have approved the ads.	The ads must have been approved.

Intransitive verbs (verbs that never have a direct object) are never used in passive voice. It is sometimes difficult to guess that a verb is intransitive. If you are unsure about a verb, use your dictionary. All dictionaries label verbs as *transitive* or *intransitive.* The verbs in the following sentences are intransitive verbs.

NOT ENGLISH Some birds are migrated north every year.
       Hydrogen is interacted by oxygen.
       Fighting is persisted between these two countries.
       Sue's birthday is coincided by our anniversary.

ENGLISH   Some birds migrate north every year.
       Oxygen interacts with hydrogen.
       Hostilities persist between these two countries.
       Our wedding anniversary coincides with Sue's birthday.

Practice Exercise

Complete each of the following sentences with a passive form of the given verb. All of the verbs in this exercise frequently occur in passive voice in academic writing.[1] Notice the prepositions that occur with these verbs.

1. estimate The number of persons with learning disabilities in the U.S.

   _____ at 15 percent of the population.

2. oblige Schools _____ by federal law to provide appropriate educational opportunities for students with disabilities.

3. document After a disability _____ by a doctor or other professional, students receive special accommodation to help them succeed in school.

4. incline In the past, schools _____ to ignore the needs of students with disabilities.

5. label Often in the past, people _____ "disabled" and then forgotten.

---

1. All the verbs in this exercise appear in the Academic and University word lists. According to Douglas Biber, Stig Johansson, Geoffrey Leech, Susan Conrad, and Edward Finegan, *The Longman Grammar of Spoken and Written English* (New York: Longman, 1999), 70 to 90 percent of the occurrences of these verbs are in passive voice in academic writing.

6. confine   For example, job opportunities for blind adults

_____ to special workshops for the blind.

7. couple   When educational opportunities _____ with employment opportunities, the lives of people with disabilities become much more satisfying and fulfilling.

8. link   Work opportunities _____ to high self-esteem.

9. design   The Americans with Disabilities Act (ADA) _____ to help all Americans participate in civic life.

10. align   The goals of the ADA _____ with the goals of most Americans.

Reasons to Use Passive Voice

Most style books (and computerized grammar checkers) say that writers should avoid passive voice because active sentences are stronger and more interesting than passive sentences. Passive sentences are more frequent in academic writing than in other kinds of English, but even in academic writing, 70 to 80 percent of the verbs are in active voice. There are, however, some good reasons to use passive voice.

Stating Generalizations

Academic writing often discusses general facts and principles instead of the actions of specific people. In the following examples, the passive sentences are stronger than the active sentences because the subjects of the active sentences are meaningless.

Active Sentence	Passive Sentence
Designers designed automobile air bags to inflate in a crash.	Automobile air bags are designed to inflate in a crash.
Workers extract oil from layers of shale.	Oil is extracted from layers of shale.
People derive many medicines from plants.	Many medicines are derived from plants.

Avoiding Blame

When people don't want to say, "I made a mistake," or, "She made a mistake," they often say, "Mistakes were made."

Avoiding Extra Long Subjects

English speakers tend to avoid really long subject noun phrases, and using the passive voice helps them do this.

Example: This report is distributed by the Multinational Investment Guarantee Agency of the World Bank Group.

Focusing Attention on the Important Information

Using passive voice sometimes allows you to focus the reader's attention on the most important information. This is often true when you are describing the steps in a process, as in the following sentences.

Active Voice	Passive Voice
The cook peels the apples, slices the apples, adds sugar, and then cooks the apples for 20 minutes.	The apples are peeled, sliced, and sugared, then cooked for 20 minutes.
Someone records the data by hand, transfers the data to a computer, and plots the data on a graph.	The data is recorded by hand, transferred to a computer, and plotted on a graph.

Increasing Coherence in Written English

Writers sometimes create a connection between sentences by ending one sentence with a noun phrase and beginning the next sentence with the same noun phrase or a synonym. This often requires making one sentence active and one sentence passive.

Examples: The vacuum tubes in radios were replaced by transistors. Transistors are much smaller and more efficient.
Lee compiled a complete set of documents. These papers were then distributed to members of the committee.

Avoiding Gendered Pronouns

Until the second half of the 20th century, writers used masculine pronouns for people in general.

Example: Each child gave his mother a rose.

Now, writers usually try to include both genders.

Example: Each child gave his or her mother a rose.

Writers sometimes use passive voice to avoid *his or her, she/he,* et cetera.

Example: Each mother was given a rose by her child.

Trouble Spots and Tricky Points

1. In many languages, passive sentences sound better (more formal, more sophisticated) than active sentences. In English, active sentences are usually stronger than passive sentences. If you don't have a good reason to use passive voice in English, don't do it.

2. In many languages, inanimate objects can't be subjects of active verbs; in English, they often are.

   Examples: The wheel of a passing truck threw a rock against my car.
   The rock hit my windshield. The windshield broke.
   An Automatic Teller Machine (ATM) dispenses money.
   The instrument panel of a car displays speed, engine temperature, and oil pressure.
   War drains money from a country's economy and displaces thousands of people.

3. In passive sentences, phrases that begin with *by* usually tell who did the action, but these phrases may also tell how or when something was done.

   Examples: The boxes were sorted by Mrs. Dye.
   The boxes were sorted by their contents.
   The boxes were sorted by 2:00 yesterday afternoon.

4. A few verbs almost always occur in passive voice.

   Examples: Walt Disney was born in 1901. (Active voice is rare but possible, as in "Mary bore a child" or "Cats bear kittens.")
   The Sears Tower is located in Chicago. (In active voice, *locate* means *find,* as in "The police located the stolen car.")
   The town is situated between tall mountains. (In active voice, *situate* means *put* or *place* and is quite rare.)

Practice Exercise

Improve the following paragraph by changing the underlined sections to passive voice.

In the United States, there are laws to protect people who have permanent disabilities. <u>The Americans with Disabilities Act (ADA) guarantees the rights of disabled persons.</u> However, the ADA doesn't deal with the World Wide Web. <u>People access the Web</u> through computer programs, and <u>programmers have developed many software programs</u> for persons with disabilities. Still, some information technology products have not been usable, and the government has instituted new regulations. Now, when <u>people develop information technology products</u> for the federal government, <u>they must make these products</u> accessible to persons with disabilities.

For Discussion and/or Writing

1. Young people are sometimes given labels, such as "the troublemaker," "the smart one," "the shy one," or "the joker." Were you ever labeled by your family or friends? How do you feel about labels? Do they create a sense of belonging? Or do they cause negative feelings?
2. Give a detailed description of a process you are studying or have studied in one of your other classes.
3. Think of a time when you were surprised by some happy event or hurt by some negative event. What happened? How do you feel about that event now?
4. Many countries have been colonized, invaded, or occupied by other countries at some time in their history. Choose such a country and briefly tell what happened to it.

REFERENCE CHART
The Longest Possible English Verb Phrase

For some students, it is helpful to see that English verb phrases follow a very organized pattern. For others, it is easier to learn verb tenses separately, one at a time. You are an expert on your own style of learning. If this chart isn't helpful to you, read it and forget it.

Subject	Verb Phrase					Object
Our cat	might	have	been	being	fed	fish.
	modal	perfect *have*	progressive *be*	passive *be*	main verb	

Notice: All of the verb tenses of English are made by choosing pieces from this verb phrase pattern, and the pieces always come in the same order.

REFERENCE CHART
A Few Other Possible Verb Phrases

Subject	Verb Phrase			Object
Our cat	has	been	eating	fish.
	perfect *have*	progressive *be*	main verb	
Our cat	was		fed	fish.
	passive *be*		main verb	
Our cat	is		eating	fish.
	progressive *be*		main verb	
Our cat	might		eat	fish.
	modal		main verb	
Our cat		eats		fish.
		main verb		

Notice:
1. If there is a marker of past or present (*is/was, has/had, does/did*, etc.) or a marker of subject-verb agreement (*do/does, have/has*, etc.), it always comes in the very first word of the verb phrase.
2. A modal is always followed by the simple form of the next verb.
3. Perfect *have* is always followed by the past participle of the next verb.
4. Progressive *be* is always followed by the present participle of the next verb.
5. Passive *be* is always followed by the past participle of the next verb.

Chapter 5
A/an and the

Introductory Focus

The words *a* and *an* are called *indefinite articles,* and *the* is called the *definite article.* Many languages do not have articles. (In fact, Old English didn't.) Other languages have articles but use them in different ways than they are used in English. Notice the use of articles in the following proverbs.

> A penny saved is a penny earned.
> Money talks.
> It is easier to make a suggestion than to carry it out.
> It is easier to give advice than to take it.
> A faithful friend is as rare as a diamond.
> A faithful friend is better than gold.
> Honesty is the first step to greatness.

Have you heard any of these sayings? What do they mean? Do you agree with them? Can you explain why *a* appears before some nouns but not before others? Why does the last proverb use *the?*

One of the following sentences uses good English. Which one is it? Can you explain why the others are not correct?

a. We discussed meaning of life.
b. We discussed the meaning of life.
c. We discussed the meaning of the life.

Many students say that languages where speakers either don't use words like *the* at all or put *the* in front of all nouns seem reasonable but that English, where speakers sometimes use *the* and sometimes don't (as in the preceding sentence *b*),[1] seem very difficult to learn. The material in this chapter may help. The first step in learning to use the definite and indefinite articles is to learn about the difference between *count nouns* and *noncount nouns.*

---

1. Sentence *b* is good English.

Count Nouns and Noncount Nouns

One of the most important distinctions in English grammar is the distinction between count and noncount nouns. These two categories of nouns behave differently in many contexts.

Count Nouns	Noncount Nouns
May be used after numbers	Are never used after numbers
May be made plural	Are never plural
Use a singular or a plural verb	Use only singular verbs
May be used after *many, few, fewer*	Are never used after *many, few, fewer*
Are never used after *much*	May be used after *much*

In addition, singular count nouns behave differently from plural count nouns and noncount nouns.

Singular Count Nouns	Plural Count Nouns and Noncount Nouns
May be used after *a/an*	Are never used after *a/an*
Never appear without a preceding article, demonstrative, or possessive	May appear without a preceding article, demonstrative, or possessive

Anyone who learns English has to learn whether a noun's meaning is count or noncount. To make matters even more complicated, many nouns have both a count and a noncount meaning. If the speaker uses the noun with grammar that goes with a count noun, the listener will get one meaning. If the speaker uses the noun with grammar that goes with a noncount noun, the listener will get a different meaning. For example:

> We have time to play golf. (We are not too busy to play golf.)
> We have a time to play golf. (We have a golf game on our schedule.)

Learning the Count/Noncount Distinction

There are three basic ways to learn whether a noun's meaning is count or noncount.

Guessing

Sometimes one can guess. For example, nouns for liquids are always noncount. *Wheat* and *rice* are noncount because, although it is possible to count the individual pieces of wheat or rice, people rarely do so; wheat and rice are measured or weighed. (If there is a need to talk about individual pieces of rice or wheat, speakers use the word *grain*.)

Using a Dictionary

It is not always possible to guess whether a noun is count or noncount, and you may need to use a dictionary. Dictionaries intended for English language learners have symbols to mark noun definitions as count or noncount.

Using Grammar Signals

Native speakers use grammar signals to tell them if a noun is count or noncount. Even very young English-speaking children are aware of these grammar signals. In one experiment, young children were shown a picture of hands squeezing together some "stuff" in a bowl. Then an adult asked either, "Can you see a sib?" or, "Can you see any sib?" The children had never heard the word *sib* before (because it wasn't an English word), but when they heard *"a sib,"* they pointed to the bowl; when they heard *"any sib,"* they pointed to the stuff in the bowl. They knew that the word *a* is a signal that the noun is something one can count and that *"any sib"* (without a plural *s* on *sib*) would refer to something one can't count.

Adult students of English can become more efficient in their learning by becoming aware of these same signals. The material in this chapter will help you learn these signals.

Identifying Count Uses of Noncount Nouns

Many—perhaps most—noncount nouns may be used as count nouns in certain circumstances. For example, *coffee* is a noncount noun in American English. However, a waiter may say, "We need two coffees at table four"; *two coffees* here refers to two cups of coffee. A specialty shop may advertise that it sells "coffees from around the world"; *coffees* here means "kinds of coffee."

English speakers turn noncount nouns into count nouns (by using *a/an* or a plural marker) to indicate a kind or type of something or to indicate a specific instance of something general.

Examples: War is hell. There were wars here in 1812 and 1860.
I hate noise. I heard a noise from the kitchen.

REFERENCE CHART
Common Noncount Nouns

Some English nouns have only count meanings; some have only noncount meanings. Many English nouns have both. This chart lists some of the most common noncount nouns.

Liquids
All nouns for liquids are noncount.

Gases
All nouns for gases are noncount, including *smog* and *air pollution*.

Things That Have Tiny Parts
Things that are usually weighed or measured, rather than counted, are predictably noncount.

wheat	salt	flour	dirt	grass	hair
rice	pepper	sugar	dust	mold	
corn	cinnamon	sand	gravel		

Solids That Can Be Cut into Smaller Pieces
This category is a little harder to predict. Several nouns in this category also have a count meaning.

bread	paper	gold	film	chalk
butter	wood	silver	glass	ice
cheese	cotton	iron		
meat				

Natural Phenomena
In their most common uses, nouns for natural phenomena are noncount, as is *pollution*.

darkness	fog	heat	lightning	snow	weather
dew	gravity	humidity	rain	sunshine	wind
electricity	hail	light	sleet	thunder	

Diseases
Nouns for diseases are usually noncount, even when the noun ends in *s*.

cancer	cholera	heart disease	measles	scabies
chicken pox	flu	malaria	rabies	smallpox

Groups Made up of Similar Individual Items
Many students say that this category is very hard to guess. There are ways to
name the individual items in these groups, but the groups themselves have
noncount names.

art	fruit	information	makeup	scenery
baggage	furniture	jewelry	merchandise	slang
cash	garbage	junk	money	traffic
change	grammar	knowledge	music	vocabulary
clothing	hardware	luggage	news	work
equipment	homework	machinery	postage	
food	housework	mail[2]	research	

Abstractions
These too may be difficult to guess. Some of the following nouns also have
count meanings, but the most common meanings are noncount.

advice	education	help	luck	sleep
anger	energy	honesty	patience	time
beauty	enjoyment	hospitality	peace	truth
behavior	evidence	importance	poverty	violence
communication	fun	intelligence	progress	wealth
confidence	happiness	justice	proof	
courage	health	love	significance	

Others
> Nouns for languages (*Arabic, Chinese, English,* etc.) are noncount.
> Nouns for fields of study (*chemistry, engineering,* etc.) are noncount,
> even if the noun ends in *s* (as in *physics, linguistics, ethics, economics,*
> *hydraulics,* etc.).
> Nouns for sports, recreational activities, and activities in general (*baseball,*
> *chess, swimming,* etc.) are noncount.

For Discussion and/or Writing

1. Emergency preparedness professionals say that we should all keep
   sufficient supplies in our homes for living for three days without help in
   case of a natural disaster, such as an earthquake or a flood, or a human-
   caused disaster, such as a chemical spill or a terrorist attack. Working with
   a partner or small group, create a list of necessary supplies for survival.
   Use numbers and plural endings with count nouns; don't use numbers or
   plural endings with noncount nouns.

---

2. Individual e-mail messages are usually treated as countable, as in "I received a lot of mail today.
I received 10 letters and 20 e-mails."

2. Imagine that you are going to prepare a special dinner for friends and that you want to include two or three of your favorite dishes. Make a shopping list for the things you will need to buy. Use numbers and plural endings with count nouns; don't use them with noncount nouns.

Article Use: Singular Count Nouns

No one has ever figured out a perfect way to explain article use in English, although linguists are trying hard to discover exactly what rules English speakers use. Some of the basic rules are well understood, however, and the most important one is this:

> Singular count nouns cannot go bare.

In almost all situations, singular count nouns must have an article or other determiner. They cannot go "bare." Even an adjective is not enough "clothing" for a singular count noun.[3] Because *book* is a singular count noun, the following sentences are not English.

> NOT ENGLISH   I read book yesterday.
> I read interesting book.

Determiners for Singular Count Nouns

Articles	Demonstratives	Possessives	Quantifiers	Numeral
a/an, the	this, that	my, our, your, her, his, its, their, Ted's, Ann's	each, every, no, any	one

Speakers and writers usually have no trouble using the words listed under *demonstratives, possessives, quantifiers,* or *numeral* in the preceding chart. The problem comes in choosing *a/an* or *the*. The following rules may help.

Rules for Choosing *a/an* or *the*

1. *A* and *an* come from the Old English word for *one;* therefore, they cannot be used with plurals or noncount nouns.
2. *A* and *an* mean "one out of many" (or at least "one out of more than one").

> *Examples:*   I bought a car. (There are lots of cars in the world. I bought one of them.)
> I bought an expensive red car. (There are lots of expensive red cars in the world. I bought one of them.)

---

3. In prepositional phrases, singular count nouns are occasionally bare. These usually have an idiomatic meaning, and some of them are discussed later in this chapter.

3. *The* means "the only one in the world" or "the only one in the little world of our conversation" (the "little world of our conversation" may be called the context or the domain of discourse), as in the following examples.

    a. She is the queen of England.
       The sun is shining.
       (There's only one in the world.)
    b. I need the blue pencil. (There are probably lots of blue pencils in the world, but in the place where we are having our conversation, there is only one blue pencil; or I want one particular pencil, and that particular pencil can be identified by its color—blue.)
    c. Give me the pencil. (There are lots of pencils in the world, but in the context of our conversation, there is only one pencil. I want it.)

Guidelines for Editing

1. Again, the most important rule is that a singular count noun cannot go bare. If a singular count noun does not have an article or other determiner before it, the sentence will not be English. There are two possible ways to correct a sentence that contains a bare count noun.

    a. Make the noun plural. (Check subject/verb agreement as needed.)
    b. Add a determiner.

    Frequently, the writer is thinking of a plural meaning, and choice *a* is the best solution. In particular, writers whose first language does not use plural endings often find that they have used a singular count noun in places where they intended a plural meaning.

2. Use the article *an* only before words that begin with a vowel sound; use the article *a* only before words that begin with a consonant sound. This is a rule for ears, not eyes.

Examples:

an apple	an elephant	an umbrella	an hour
a pear	a giraffe	a union	a history

Practice Exercises

1. Write an *E* in the blank before each sentence that contains a bare singular count noun.

    ___ a. Jon's analysis of problem is weak.
    ___ b. We put gasoline in the car yesterday.
    ___ c. Pam is a prime suspect in murder case.

___ d. Ann does not know result of the laboratory experiment.

___ e. The project may be slow because they are pursuing difficult goal.

___ f. Children may be harmed if they are exposed to intense violence in movies.

___ g. The project will probably run into complication later on.

___ h. Children develop asthma more often when there is smog in the air.

___ i. The committee reached conclusion that pollution is increasing.

___ j. Distinctive feature of this car is its low price.

2. Edit the following sentences, correcting any errors in noun phrases. There may be more than one way to correct a sentence, and one or more sentences do not contain an error. Discuss the reasons for your choices.

a. Jan was sole survivor of the accident.

b. Please comply with request from the central management office.

c. Honesty and hard work are element of good business administration.

d. It is important that patient consult physician before taking drug.

e. If they wish to keep mistake to minimum, supervisor must get information to employee quickly and accurately.

f. We made fundamental mistake at the beginning of our project.

g. In different context, this sentence would have a very different meaning.

h. U.S. companies import supplies from many regions.

i. In similar way, it is important to publish report on the environmental impact of project before the project begins.

j. New information will ultimately lead us to formulate new hypothesis.

Article Use: Plurals and Noncount Nouns

Unlike singular count nouns, noncount nouns and plural count nouns can sometimes go "bare." An article or other determiner is not always required in front of these nouns. For example, the following sentences are good English.

I read books every day.
We need time and money.

Frequently, however, plurals and noncount nouns do use a determiner.

Determiners for Plurals

Articles	Demonstratives	Possessives	Quantifiers	Numerals
the	these, those	my, our, your, her, his, its, their, Ted's, Ann's	all, both, many, most, a few, some, several, no, any	two, three, 100

Determiners for Noncount Nouns

Articles	Demonstratives	Possessives	Quantifiers
the	this, that	my, our, your, her, his, its, their, Ted's, Ann's	all, much, most, any, some, little, no

Speakers and writers usually have no trouble using the words listed under *demonstratives, possessives, quantifiers,* or *numerals* in the preceding charts. The difficulty usually comes in choosing whether to use *the* or nothing at all. The following rules may help.

Rules for Choosing *the* or ∅ (No Article)

1. Use no article with a plural or noncount noun if it refers to the stuff (things, substance, idea) in general.
2. Use *the* to refer to a particular subset of the stuff.

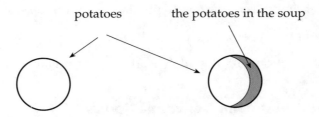

potatoes   the potatoes in the soup

    a. Potatoes are nutritious. (potatoes in general)
    b. The potatoes in this soup are soft. (some particular potatoes)
    c. I usually like coffee, but I don't like the coffee Kim makes. (I like coffee in general, but I don't like this particular coffee.)
    d. I need money. (Any money is fine.)
    e. I want the money you owe me. (I want some particular money, the money you owe me.)

In the following sentences, the speaker wants the listener to understand that the plural or noncount noun refers to a particular subset. The subset includes all of the stuff (things, substance, idea) important in the context of the conversation, but not the stuff in general.

    a. I don't like this city, because the air smells awful. (*The air* refers to the air in the city, not all air.)

    b. I threw away my shirt because the sleeves were worn out. (The sleeves on my shirt were worn out, not all sleeves in general.)

    c. Tell me the truth! (I want a true answer to a question I have asked. I don't want you to discuss philosophical truth in general.)

Practice Exercises

1. Edit the following sentences, correcting any errors in noun phrases. There may be more than one way to correct a sentence. Discuss the reasons for your choices.

    a. Philip Mazzei played crucial role in the American Revolution.

    b. The professor raised valid point at committee meeting yesterday.

    c. Did Ron acquire cars in his garage legally?

    d. Principle of marketing is that music helps sell merchandise.

    e. There is intense magnetic field near the North Pole.

    f. Critic said yesterday's performance showed both intelligence and immense energy.

    g. In basketball game, referee must be neutral and not favor one team or other.

    h. This lecture will focus on meaning of statistics about population growth.

    i. Tax policies inhibit the growth of computer company in some countries.

    j. Capital is important factor underlying economic growth.

2. Accuracy practice: Compose sentences using the following words. Do not change the order of the words, but add words or change any word forms as necessary.

   a. I / need / information / about / computer / code

   b. institution / receive / money / for research / malaria

   c. Lee / present / analysis / of / situation

   d. horizontal / axis / represent / time

   e. we / try / find / source / of / problem

3. Edit the following paragraph, correcting any errors in noun phrases. There is more than one way to correct the paragraph. Discuss the reasons for your choices.

   During the past decade, developments in computer industry have had an immense impact on libraries. Not long ago, most libraries maintained card catalog of their holdings. Each time library added book to its collection, someone typed card telling title, author, and subject of book, as well as other information. These cards were then filed alphabetically in the drawers of large cabinet. Library patron who wished to find books on particular subject searched through the drawers of cabinet, and librarians held classes for patron teaching them how to use card catalog. Such system now seems extremely unsophisticated. Library's holdings are now listed in computer database. The database includes information on not only the subject, author, and title of book but also its status (whether it is on shelves or checked out and, if checked out, its due date). In addition, libraries now have databases with information about article found inside books and journal. Librarians continue to hold classes for patron, but the classes are now about how to use computer.

For Discussion and/or Writing

1. Imagine that you have an opportunity to interview one of your heroes. (This could be one of your intellectual heroes or someone famous in movies or other media.) Write a list of 10 questions you can ask about your hero's interests, experiences, and hopes for the future. Pay careful attention to article use.
2. Imagine that you are an architect who is designing a very luxurious apartment for a wealthy client. Describe in detail what luxuries you will include in the apartment. Pay careful attention to article use.

Generic Use of Nouns

Sometimes nouns are used to refer in a general way to an entire group or class. This is called *generic use.*

Guidelines for Generic Use

1. You should leave generic noncount nouns bare.

   Examples: Carbon monoxide is a colorless, odorless, and very poisonous gas.
   Embroidery is the art of decorating fabric with needlework.

2. You should usually make generic count nouns plural.

   Examples: Locomotives are self-propelled engines that move railcars on tracks.
   Giraffes are ruminant mammals with long necks and legs.

3. Technical writing sometimes uses a singular count noun with *a/an* or *the* for generic meaning. This is a matter of style. Again, the most important rule is that a singular count noun cannot go bare.

   Examples: A giraffe is a ruminant mammal from Africa.
   The giraffe is a ruminant African mammal.

Practice Exercise

Generic use often occurs in definitions. Write definitions for the following words.

a. hereditary trait

b. bond

c. entrepreneur

d. contamination

e. computer

f. sonnet

g. money

Helpful Guidelines

First Mention, Second Mention Rule

Often, the first mention of a singular count noun in a text requires *a/an* (*some* for plurals and noncount nouns), and the second mention of the noun requires *the.*

Example: Choose a card. Now turn the card over.

The first sentence says to pick any card out of all the cards available. Once this is done, the conversation is limited to one card. The second sentence talks about that one card. (Another way to look at it is to say that the first mention establishes a subset of all the objects in the world; the second mention, using *the,* points to that subset.)

Nouns Made Specific in the Text

If a noun is further defined or limited in the text, it is very often preceded by *the*. (The additional information limits the noun to a subset of the group/substance/stuff in general.)

Examples: the books on the table
the books that I read last year
the information that you need
the woman who wrote this book

Shared Resources

When a community or group (family, etc.) shares an object or resource, English speakers usually use *the* when referring to the object or resource. At one time, there was usually only one doctor in a town; now, there may be many doctors in a town, but people still say, "I went to the doctor yesterday." Until very recently, houses did not have indoor plumbing, much less multiple bathrooms. Today, even if there are two or three bathrooms in a house, people say, for example, "Sue is in the bathroom brushing her teeth."

Examples: *the store, the library, the kitchen, the newspaper*
Please put the newspaper in the kitchen before you go to the store.
I heard on the radio that the police arrested two men at the library today.

Proper Names

English-speaking cultures generally have very few rules about names; therefore, proper names come in many forms, and the only safe rule is to learn each name individually. A glance through the business directory of one community found all of the following business names.

Lamonts Apparel	The Athlete's Foot	That Pizza Place
Claire's Pantry	The Talbots	That's Sharp
Auntie Anne's	The Gap	A Better Telephone Shop

Geographic Names

Names of rivers and oceans usually use *the*. Names of lakes, islands, and mountains usually don't. Names of groups of mountains, groups of islands, or "plural" countries use *the*. (A "plural" country is a country whose name indicates that it is comprised of a group of smaller states.)

Examples:

the Columbia River	the Amazon
the Indian Ocean	the Pacific
the Ural Mountains	the Appalachians
the Hawaiian Islands	the Azores
the United States	the United States of America
the United Arab Emirates	the Philippines

the United Kingdom of Great Britain and Northern Ireland

But:

Crater Lake	Ellis Island	Mount Rainier	Venezuela
Lake Michigan	Long Island	Mount Olympus	Japan

Partitive Expressions

Partitive expressions refer to part of something and begin with *some of, part of, all of, three of,* et cetera. Partitive expressions do not allow bare nouns of any kind. They usually use *the.*[4]

Examples: some of the apples
part of the time
all of the children

(*All children* and *all the children* are good English, but with the partitive expression *all of,* the phrase must be *all of the children.*)

Prepositional Phrases

Prepositional phrases sometimes have special meanings that allow a bare count noun. It is probably easiest to treat these as idiomatic. Here are some examples: *She is in school* means that she is participating in the activity of getting an education; *she is in the school* means that she is inside the school building. *He goes to church* means that he participates in the activities, worship, et cetera, of a church; *he went to the church* means that he went to the church building (perhaps to use the copy machine). Use *the* for a location and ∅ (nothing) for an activity.

The prepositions *from* and *to* sometimes allow a bare count noun when they are used in the pattern *from A to B* or *between A and B*. It may be necessary to ask a native speaker for guidance.

---

4. The expression *a lot of* is sometimes partitive and sometimes not. Speakers usually use *a lot of* instead of *much* in positive statements, as in "She has a lot of money." Speakers use either *a lot of* or *much* in negative statements, as in "We don't have a lot of time" and "We don't have much time." This use of *a lot of* is not partitive.

Examples: with brotherhood from sea to shining sea
handed down from mother to daughter
communication between brother and sister
division of responsibility between city and state

Job Titles

When a phrase can be interpreted as either a job description or a position title, the speaker may often choose whether or not to use *the.*

Examples: Abraham Lincoln, president of the United States, signed this letter.
Abraham Lincoln, the president of the United States, signed this letter.

Idiomatic Use

Some uses of *the* are best treated as idiomatic. Sometimes you just have to ask a native speaker for guidance.

Practice Exercises

1. Edit the following sentences, correcting any errors in noun phrases. There may be more than one way to correct a sentence. Discuss the reasons for your choices.

   a. The repair crew needs accurate diagram of plane's interior.

   b. The dean rejected some recommendations but accepted recommendation from the student committee.

   c. This calculation is based on speed of light.

   d. Store manager selected the winning number for contest at random.

   e. In particular context, this action may constitute a felony.

   f. There is explicit rule against disposing of chemical in the lab sinks.

   g. It is not appropriate for child to use motorized vehicle.

   h. Plot to overthrow government was reported by credible news agency today.

   i. None of other planets in this solar system have large amounts of surface water.

2. Edit the following paragraphs. There may be more than one way to correct the noun phrases. Discuss the reasons for your choices.

Principle of free speech has been an important concept throughout history of United States. Many people argue that maintaining uninhibited free speech is crucial to maintaining our existence as democracy and to maintaining creative spirit within our culture. Others argue that some limits on free speech are appropriate and necessary for protection of individuals.

Those who advocate limits on free speech frequently cite hate speech as category of speech that should be controlled. They argue that songs and films filled with racial insults are capable of causing significant harm to individuals and that glorification of violence that is found in much contemporary music is dangerous to community. Supreme Court has ruled in past that freedom of speech ends when it creates a clear and present danger to others. Advocates of limits maintain that singing about how good it feels to kill police or to burn down ethnic grocery stores is analogous to falsely shouting, "Fire!" in crowded building. It is dangerous and should be illegal.

Others argue against such limits. They argue that if we place restrictions on what individual are allowed to say, we run risk of inhibiting creativity of artists and of suppressing important discussions. If the government is allowed to decide what words or ideas are considered dangerous or insulting, soon any criticism of the government may be labeled "insulting" and banned. If artist are not allowed to say, write, or sing about hatred and violence, we may not find out what some people are thinking. It is better to expose negative idea and argue against them than to suppress them.

For Discussion and/or Writing

1. Choose a city and describe one of the following. Pay careful attention to article use:

   Traffic conditions
   The educational system
   A local festival or holiday
   Housing patterns

2. Describe some of the important steps a student can take to prepare for attending a university. Pay careful attention to article use.

3. What do you think are the most important things that money can't buy? What are some important things that require money? Again, pay careful attention to article use.

Chapter 6
Subject-Verb Agreement

Introductory Focus

Many learners say that the problem of subject-verb agreement is one of the more annoying details of English. Look at the following proverbs.

There is no fun like work.
The best things in life are free.
Bad news travels fast.
April showers bring May flowers.

Do you understand these sayings? Do you agree with them? Notice the forms of the verbs. What is the difference between *is* and *are?* Why is there an *s* on *travels?*

Agreement

The subject of a clause determines the form of a verb.

The verb *be* is very irregular.

Simple Present		Simple Past	
I am	we are	I was	we were
you are[1]	you are	you were	you were
she, he, it is	they are	she, he, it was	they were

---

1. In Early Modern English, such as the English in Shakespeare's writings and in the King James translation of the Bible, you will see *thou art*. This was a second person singular form.

For other verbs, in the simple present tense, third person singular subjects require an *s* on the end of the verb. (Third person means anything that is not *I, we,* or *you.*)

Examples: Our <u>office uses</u> an old version of this word-processing software.
Other <u>offices use</u> newer versions of the software.
<u>Sue dislikes</u> the virtual desktop on her computer screen.
<u>I like</u> to explore virtual reality through computers.

Many language learners have trouble remembering to add the *s* to third person singular verbs. In one way, this is not a big problem. No one will ever misunderstand the meaning of a sentence if you forget the *s.* In another way, this is a very big problem. When university professors are asked what language errors bother them the most, they say that a missing *s* is very highly annoying. Perhaps this is because the third person singular *s* is a marker of social status. Traditionally, people who say *he don't* and *she go* instead of *he doesn't* and *she goes* have been considered uneducated.

Troublesome Subjects

The rules for subject-verb agreement occasionally cause problems even for native speakers. The following sections discuss some of the trouble spots.

There as a Subject

In writing, when *there* is a subject, the verb agrees with the noun in the predicate.

Examples: There is a table in the kitchen.
There are four chairs around the table.
There is some water on the floor.
There's not very much space in the cupboard.

In informal speech, people often use *there's* with plural nouns.

Examples: There's some apples on the table.
There's some questions that we need to discuss.

This is not acceptable in academic writing.

Practice Exercise

Accuracy practice: Compose sentences using the following words. Do not change the order of the words, but add words or change any word forms as necessary.

a. there / good news / today

b. there / many / alternative / routes / for commuters

c. there / an earlier version of this software / on / Lee / computer

d. there / garbage / street / after / parade

e. there / three / motive / for the crime

Unusual Singular and Plural Forms

A few English words use Latin plural forms. Because these plural forms don't end in *s*, they are easy to miss.

Examples:

Singular	Plural
criterion	criteria
datum	data
medium	media
phenomenon	phenomena
radius	radii
stratum	strata

The words *data* and *media* are treated as noncount nouns by many speakers and used with singular verbs.

A few nouns have only a plural form. These words use a plural verb.

Examples: police (Use *police officer* for the singular.)
people (Use *person* for the singular.)
clothes
cattle

A few nouns have only a plural form, but using *a pair of* makes them countable. These words use a plural verb when they stand alone.

Examples: *eyeglasses, pants, scissors*
These pants are dirty.
This pair of pants is torn.

A few words have one spelling for both the singular and the plural forms. These words use a singular verb when the meaning is singular and a plural verb when the meaning is plural.

Examples: *series, species, fish, sheep, deer*
A new television series begins next Monday.
Two new series begin next Tuesday.

Practice Exercise

Complete each of the following sentences with the correct form of the verb in parentheses.

a. These criteria _____ (seem) to be important.

b. This species _____ (need) protection.

c. Many species _____ (be) endangered.

d. My scissors _____ (have) blue handles.

e. A new pair of scissors _____ (be) on order.

Coordinated Subjects

When a subject has two equal parts joined by *and* or *or/nor,* it is called a *coordinated subject* or a *compound subject.* These subjects often cause problems even for native speakers.

And

If the noun phrases (singular or plural) are joined with *and,* use a plural verb.

Examples: The appendix and the index to this book are at the back.
The table of contents and the notes to teachers and students are at the front.

If the two noun phrases combine to create one entity, writers often use a singular verb.

Example: Scrambled eggs and toast is my favorite breakfast.
Scrambled eggs and toast are my favorite breakfast foods.

Or/nor

If two singular noun phrases are joined with *or* or *nor,* use a singular verb.

Examples: Either Dan or Sue is going to teach the tennis class this afternoon.
Neither cold weather nor rain poses a problem for an indoor tennis game.

If two plural noun phrases are joined with *or* or *nor,* use a plural verb.

Examples: Are either the players or their parents cooperating with the coaches?
Neither the players nor the coaches want to practice outdoors today.

If a plural noun is joined to a singular noun with *or* or *nor,* some style guides suggest making the verb agree with the closest noun.

Examples: Neither the players nor the coach has been given the new schedule.
Either the coach or the players have been damaging the tennis court.

Other professional writers say that you should avoid this kind of sentence. Statistically, most speakers use a singular verb in these constructions.

Practice Exercise

Complete each of the following sentences with the correct present tense form of the verb in parentheses.

a. Neither the intermediate students nor the advanced students

_____ (use) these dictionaries.

b. Either the librarian or the principal _____ (choose) dictionaries for the school.

c. The teachers and the librarian _____ (want) students to utilize computer-based dictionaries.

Prepositional Phrases in Subjects

Some subject noun phrases include one or more prepositional phrases after the main noun. The main noun is the subject of the sentence. Don't be confused by the nouns in the prepositional phrases. (Standardized tests often use long prepositional phrases to confuse test takers.)

Examples: The orientation <u>program</u> for new students <u>takes</u> about three hours.

The <u>prospects</u> for finding a suitable replacement for the former teacher of the first year mathematics class <u>are</u> not good.

Partitive expressions, such as *three of the books* or *some of the milk,* refer to part of a group or part of a quantity. Subject-verb agreement depends on whether the noun is count or noncount. Noncount and singular count nouns use singular verbs.[2]

Examples: <u>Some</u> of this technology <u>is</u> quite new.
<u>Some</u> of these techniques <u>are</u> quite new.
<u>All</u> of the region <u>is</u> economically depressed.
<u>All</u> of the students <u>are</u> depressed about their grades.
<u>One</u> of the companies <u>has</u> ceased operations.
<u>Three</u> of the companies <u>have</u> continued operating.

---

2. Native speakers argue about subject-verb agreement when *none* is used in a partitive expression. One rule says to use a singular verb (e.g., "None of the boys is happy").

The Number, a Number, the Percentage, a Percentage

When the subject is *the number* or *the percentage*, use a singular verb.

Examples: The <u>number</u> of companies in this category <u>appears</u> small.
The annual <u>percentage</u> of business failures <u>is</u> declining.

When the subject is *a number*, use a plural verb.

Examples: A <u>number</u> of businesses <u>have</u> closed.
A <u>number</u> of employees <u>need</u> help.

When the subject is *a percentage*, subject-verb agreement depends on whether the noun is count or noncount.

Examples: A large <u>percentage</u> of the workers <u>are</u> seeking new jobs.
A small <u>percentage</u> of the workforce <u>is</u> relying on government benefits.

Practice Exercise

Complete each of the following sentences with the correct form of the verb in parentheses.

a. The dimensions of the room _____ (be) quite small.

b. The size of these rooms _____ (be) inadequate for our needs.

c. Some of Americans' most important civil rights _____ (be) guaranteed in the first 10 amendments to the U.S. Constitution.

d. Some of the information in this book _____ (seem) out of date.

e. All modes of transportation _____ (require) energy.

f. The number of modes of transportation that can be supported by the infrastructure of a developing country and integrated into its internal

transportation system _____ (be) limited.

g. A number of scholars _____ (have) given input on this transportation proposal.

For Discussion and/or Writing

1. A dynamic person is full of energy and new ideas; a dull person is boring and has no imagination. Sal is dynamic; Syl is dull. What do you think Sal and Syl do each day? Why do you suppose people think that Sal is dynamic and that Syl is dull?

2. In the past, only a very small percentage of the U.S. population ever attended college. Currently, a large portion of the population attends college for at least a few terms. In your opinion, why has this change occurred? What do you think the future trends will be?

3. Basic research often seems slow and unproductive, but without it, more profitable applications are not possible. Describe an instance where basic research has paid off in benefits for humanity. What was the research? What are the results today?

Chapter 7
Modifiers and Comparisons

Introductory Focus

Adjectives and other modifiers help make the meaning of a noun phrase exact. Look at the following proverbs and sayings.

> A good conscience is a soft pillow.
> Ignorance of the law is no excuse.
> A contented person is never poor; a discontented person is never rich.
> Experience is the best teacher.
> The pen is mightier than the sword.

Do you understand these sayings? Do you agree with them? Find the noun phrases. Notice the words and phrases that modify the nouns.

Noun phrases can go in several places in sentences. (For simplicity, when a noun stands alone, it may be called a very short noun phrase.)

Subject	That new microscope is very useful.
Direct object	Our school bought a small telescope.
Indirect object	A kind donor gave the library a large, expensive globe.
Complement	Mr. Kim is the school's purchasing agent.
Object of a preposition	Schools must spend money on laboratory equipment.

Modifiers of Nouns

Nouns can be modified in many ways: by one-word adjectives, by another noun, by a phrase, or by a clause.

Examples: I bought a big, green book.
I bought a chemistry book.
I bought a book with a green cover.
I bought a book about chemistry.
I bought a book that I need for my chemistry class.

The general rule in English is: "light" modifiers go in front of a noun, and "heavy" modifiers go after a noun. A single word is "light." A phrase or clause is "heavy." Notice the location of the various kinds of modifiers in the preceding examples.

Descriptive Adjectives

When English speakers use more than one adjective before a noun, the adjectives usually follow a particular order: opinion—physical properties—origin—material. This is not a strict rule of English, but your writing will sound a little more natural if you follow this order for adjectives.

Examples: my pretty little Chinese silk purse
these beautiful simulated Italian leather gloves

Adjectives for physical properties usually follow this order: size—shape—condition—age—color.

Example: my big, bulky, worn-out, old blue coat

Writers sometimes put three or four modifiers in front of a noun, but they usually use only one or two. Sometimes, two adjectives are joined with the word *and,* especially if the two adjectives are from the same category (e.g., silk and rayon).

Quantifiers

Quantifiers are a special kind of adjective that tell the amount (quantity) of a noun. The most important ones are *all, both, each, every, many, much, most, a few, some, several, no,* and *any.* Quantifiers come first, before other adjectives, in noun phrases. Some quantifiers go with count nouns; other quantifiers go with noncount nouns. (See pp. 61–64.)

Attributive Nouns

In English, nouns are often used to modify other nouns.[1] It is perfectly correct to say, for example, *the legs of the table* or *the handle of the door*, but people very often say *the table legs* and *the door handle* instead. If you use a great many *of* phrases and very few noun-noun combinations, your writing will have a little bit of a foreign "accent."

In noun-noun combinations, the first noun is always in its singular form.

> NOT ENGLISH   a files cabinet
>   a flowers vase

Practice Exercise

Change the following phrases into noun-noun combinations. All the phrases that you create will be common combinations.

a. a monitor for a computer

b. a series for television

c. the cycle of life

d. a range of mountains

e. a decline in the stock market

f. a symbol of status

g. a tax on income

h. a tax on an estate

i. a highlight of a movie

j. a statement of vision

Participial Adjectives

The pieces of verb phrases that are usually called *present participles* (*-ing* forms, such as *walking, sleeping, talking*) and the pieces of verb phrases that are usually called *past participles* (*-ed* forms, such as *invited* and *defeated*, or irregular forms, such as *known* and *broken*) have taken on additional jobs in

---

1. Some books call these *attributive nouns*. Other books call them a kind of *compound noun*.

English. Sometimes these pieces of verbs are employed as adjectives. Some examples are shown in the following chart.

Participle	Verb Phrase with Participle	Participial Adjective
known	We <u>have known</u> about the meeting for weeks.	Tom is a <u>known</u> criminal.
damaged	Lightning <u>has damaged</u> the building.	The <u>damaged</u> cars were towed away.
invited	Sue <u>was invited</u> to speak at the conference.	The <u>invited</u> guests have arrived.
sleeping	The dog <u>is sleeping</u>.	The <u>sleeping</u> children are cute.
talking	I <u>am talking</u> to Sue.	Sue has a <u>talking</u> doll.
damaging	The wind <u>is damaging</u> the trees.	A <u>damaging</u> wind blew trees down.

Occasionally, too, participial adjectives are formed from phrasal verbs. For example, an *upcoming event* is an event that is coming up (happening) soon. A *forthcoming book* is a book that will be published soon. You will see a few adjectives that include an adverb with the participial. A *well-adjusted child* is a child who has adjusted well to life. If someone refers to a *so-called great idea,* the speaker means that people call it a great idea (but the speaker probably disagrees).

Deciding whether to use the past participle form or the present participle form as an adjective is sometimes difficult. The basic rule is:

a. The present participle form (the *-ing* form) has an active meaning. (*Sleeping children* are *children who are sleeping. A damaging wind is a wind that damages things.*) Sometimes the action is not yet completed. (*A gathering crowd* is a group of people who are still walking into an area.)

b. The past participle form has a passive meaning. (*Damaged cars* are *cars that were damaged* by someone else.) The action is completed. (*A gathered crowd* is a group of people who are standing together.)

Admittedly, there are times when this rule is difficult to interpret; however, participial adjectives usually follow these principles.

Practice Exercise

Complete the following story with adjectives formed from the verbs in parentheses.

Sue and Tom finished cleaning the room and looked around happily at the neatly _____ (sweep) floor and the _____ (polish) wood furniture in their cozy living room. _____ (sparkle) sunshine came in through the newly _____ (wash) windows with their neatly _____ (iron) curtains. In the kitchen, there were loaves of bread in the oven. Tom and Sue could smell the _____ (bake) loaves and knew that soon they would eat freshly _____ (bake) bread. The look on their _____ (smile) faces said that they were a very happy couple.

When participial adjectives are formed from verbs of emotion, the present participial (-*ing* form) describes the person or thing that causes the emotion. (An *exciting movie* causes a feeling of excitement.) The past participial (-*ed* or an irregular form) describes the person who feels the emotion. (An *excited child* feels a lot of excitement.)

Practice Exercise

Complete the following sentences with participial adjectives.

1. The professor's lecture confused the students. The students experienced a lot of confusion while they listened to the lecture.

   a. The lecture was very _____. It was a _____ lecture.

   b. The students felt _____. They were _____ students.

2. The storm frightened the children. The children felt a lot of fear.

   a. The children felt _____. They were very _____ children.

   b. The storm seemed _____. It was a _____ storm.

3. The news surprised the people. The people had a big surprise when they read the news.

    a. The news was quite _____. It was _____ news.

    b. The people were _____. They acted like _____ people.

4. Sue loves her baby very much. She gives her baby lots of love.

    a. Sue is very _____ to her baby. She is a _____ mother.

    b. The baby is definitely a well- _____ child.

In many cases, participial adjectives have become part of standard phrases in English, and speakers rarely think about the form of such adjectives. Many English speakers say they give their plants *tender loving care,* but not many speakers stop to wonder whether *care* can *love* anything, especially a plant. If someone says, "Sue had a *knowing smile* on her face," the speaker means that the smile showed that Sue knew all about a situation. Speakers learn phrases like these by hearing and reading them frequently.

Practice Exercise

Complete each of the following sentences with an adjective formed from the given verb. In each case, the phrase you create will be a common collocation in English.

    1. acquire   Appreciation for lutefisk[2] is an _____ taste.

    2. fragment   Lack of coordination between government agencies resulted in a _____ response to the problems of small communities in the mountains.

    3. justify   Community leaders are expressing a lot of _____ anger about the government's lack of response to these problems.

    4. unify   Leaders should work together and take a _____ approach to problems.

    5. dominate   Protecting salmon is the _____ concern of our organization.

---

2. Lutefisk is a traditional Norwegian dish made by treating dried codfish with lye.

6. isolate   This accident is the only one that has happened, so I think it is an _____ incident.

7. pollute   Fish can't live in a _____ stream.

8. restrain   The judge issued a _____ order to stop people from polluting the river.

9. assemble   Dr. Lee discussed the judge's order with the _____ group.

10. predict   Our publicity campaign did not meet with the _____ response, because no one listened to our ads.

Adverbs

Many adverbs modify verbs, and some adverbs modify adjectives, clauses, or other constructions. The adverbs in the following sentences are underlined.

> The police <u>very quickly</u> traced the stolen car to Tom's garage.
> Dan contacted the police <u>immediately</u>.
> Dan was <u>visibly</u> upset.
> <u>Apparently</u>, Dan's car was stolen.

Frequency Adverbs

Some adverbs tell how often something happens. Although these adverbs are sometimes at the beginning or end of a clause, they usually occur in the middle of a clause (but never between the verb and its object). Notice the placement of these frequency adverbs.

Subject	First Auxiliary or Main Verb *Be*	Frequency Adverb	Other Auxiliaries, Main Verb, Object	Rest of Predicate
Money	is	never		equal to happiness.
Health	has	often	been called	wealth.
Adults	can	usually	discriminate	between money and love.
Children		sometimes	equate gifts	with love.

Adverbs of Degree and Emphasis

Some adverbs modify adjectives and other adverbs and either strengthen or weaken their meaning. Academic writers must be precise and accurate, so they often use adverbs to modify their statements. The following list includes some of the adverbs that academic writers use.

very	fairly	almost	relatively
quite	rather	nearly	
completely	somewhat	slightly	
enormously			
extremely			
highly			
really			
strongly			
supremely			

The words in the first column are also used with *not*. The word *relatively* means "in comparison with other situations" and is a very frequently used word.

Examples: Because we had done very little research on the subject, our decision to buy this kind of copy machine was somewhat arbitrary.
We are relatively sure that we made a good decision.
Ann's decision was based on scientific facts and was completely rational.

Practice Exercise

Working with a partner, tell a little about yourself by completing each of the following sentences with an adverb of degree or emphasis.

Example: I am not completely happy today.

a. I am _____ happy today.

b. I am _____ athletic.

c. I am _____ busy this week.

d. I am _____ satisfied with my living situation.

e. I am _____ interested in . . .

Very, Too, and *Enough*

Language learners often have trouble with these three common adverbs.

Very means "strongly," "a lot this way."

Too means "excessive," "more than it should be." Speakers often use *too* to express a negative judgement. If you use *too* when you mean *very*, people will think you are complaining or unhappy.

Notice the difference in these two sentences.

> It is very hot today. (a factual statement)
> It is too hot today. (a complaint)

Too phrases are often used with an infinitive (*to* + VERB).

Examples: Jan is too sad and worried to enjoy a movie right now.
               The theater was too noisy for us to enjoy the film.

Very phrases are not used with an infinitive.

> NOT ENGLISH   I am very tired to study.
>
> ENGLISH   I am too tired to study.

Enough means "sufficient," "the amount that we need." It is used after adjectives or adverbs and either before or after nouns. It is often followed by an infinitive.

Examples: We have time enough to see a movie, but we don't have enough
               money to buy tickets.
               Pat is mature enough to understand this film.
               If we walk quickly enough, we will get to the theater on time.

Practice Exercise

Complete the following sentences in ways that make good sense.

a. I am not rich enough . . .

b. I am strong enough . . .

c. Jan is too smart . . .

d. My town is too _____ to . . .

For Discussion and/or Writing

1. Give a detailed description of a car, a garden, or a pet that you would like to have.
2. Tell about a frightening, exciting, or inspiring event in your life. What happened? How did you feel at the time? What do you think about the experience now?
3. A happy, contented life usually includes some external factors (e.g., enough food, adequate housing) and some internal factors (e.g., a positive attitude, self-acceptance). What, in your opinion, are the most important factors in a happy life?

Comparisons

Some adjectives and adverbs are *gradable*. For example, *easy* is gradable, because something can be more or less easy. *Unique* and *concurrent* are not gradable. If something is unique, it has no equal; it is the only one of its kind. Most careful writers do not say *more unique* or *very unique*. If two things happen *concurrently*, they happen at the same time. Although events may happen *nearly concurrently* or *almost concurrently*, they never happen *more concurrently*.

Gradable adjectives and adverbs have comparative and superlative forms. The following chart shows the rules for forming them.

Adjective	Comparative	Superlative
One syllable	*-er*	*(the) + -est*
big	bigger	(the) biggest
high	higher	(the) highest
Two or more syllables	*more*	*(the) most*
efficient	more efficient	(the) most efficient
significant	more significant	(the) most significant
Ending in *-y* or *-le*	*-er*	*(the) + -est*
early	earlier	(the) earliest
simple	simpler	(the) simplest

Adverb	Comparative	Superlative
One syllable	*-er*	*-est*
hard	harder	(the) hardest
fast	faster	(the) fastest
Ending with *-ly*	*more*	*most*
consistently	more consistently	(the) most consistently
importantly	more importantly	most importantly

Notice:

1. The comparative form is used to compare two things; the superlative form is used to compare three or more things.
2. The words *less* and *least* are the opposites of *more* and *most*.
3. Speakers sometimes use *more* and *most* with one- and two-syllable adjectives (e.g., *more fair, more likely*). The rules for two-syllable adjectives aren't rigid, and there is some variation in the forms.
4. Superlative forms usually need *the,* but if an adverb modifies a complete sentence, *the* is not used.

   Examples: Most importantly, we must never violate our ethical standards. Most frequently, these meetings run late.

5. The words *good, well,* and *bad* are completely irregular. The forms are

   good, better, (the) best
   well, better, (the) best
   bad, worse, (the) worst
   badly, worse, (the) worst

Comparative Sentences

Comparative sentences use *than*. Both of the following sentences are correct.

   Ann is taller than Sue.
   Ann is taller than Sue is.

If two things are equal, you can use the pattern *as . . . as.*

Examples: Ann is as tall as Sue.
Ann is as tall as Sue is.
Tom works as quickly as Ron.
Tom works as quickly as Ron does.

Practice Exercise

Complete each of the following sentences with a correct form of the modifier in parentheses.

a. The president's approach to the problem was _____ (simple) the mayor's approach.

b. The president's approach was _____ (straightforward) the mayor's approach.

c. The mayor's suggestion was _____ (complicated) of all the suggestions.

d. My suggestion is _____ (good) the mayor's suggestion.

e. The mayor's idea is _____ (bad) idea that I have ever heard.

f. I am _____ (intelligent) the mayor.

Because they must be accurate and precise, academic writers often use an adverb to modify a comparison. Instead of using the formula *A is larger than B,* they use the formulas *A is somewhat larger than B* and *A is slightly larger than B.* Adverbs that can be used this way include the following:

dramatically	appreciably	considerably	slightly	apparently
obviously	perceptibly	somewhat	marginally	
definitely	noticeably		minimally	
	visibly			

The word *apparently* is often used like *noticeably* or *visibly,* to mean that something can be observed with one's senses and seems to be true, but it also means that the speaker believes further research may change this opinion. *Apparently* may be used to modify a complete clause.

Examples: The location of an advertisement is apparently more important than the size of an advertisement.
Apparently, location is considerably more important than size.

Practice Exercise

Use the data in the table to complete the following sentences. Use adverbs to modify the comparisons.

Used Car	Jaguar Sedan	Lexus Sedan	Cadillac Sedan	Dodge SUV	Land Rover SUV	Ford SUV
Price	$36,500	$40,500	$31,800	$23,465	$36,865	$28,400

1. The Jaguar is _____ (expensive) the Land Rover.

2. The Dodge is _____ (cheap) the Lexus.

3. The Dodge is _____ (cheap) the Ford.

4. The Lexus is _____ (expensive) the Cadillac.

The More . . . the More

English has an idiomatic construction that uses comparative forms. This construction is very unusual (there is no main verb in the sentence), but it is also widely used.[3]

Sentence	Meaning
The more I study, the more I learn.	If I study a little bit more, I learn a little bit more. If I study a lot more, I learn a lot more.
The more carefully he works, the fewer errors he makes.	If he works carefully, he makes few errors. If he works very carefully, he makes fewer errors.
The bigger the house, the bigger the heating bill.	If a house is big, it has a big heating bill. If a house is very big, it has a very big heating bill.

3. This construction comes from over 1,500 years ago, when English had an instrumental case marker for nouns. This use of *the* comes from a word that meant *"by the amount."*

Practice Exercise

Complete the following sentences:

a. The more I speak English, . . .

b. The more money I have, . . .

c. The harder I work, . . .

For Discussion and/or Writing

1. Who is your favorite musician, athlete, movie star, or writer? In what ways is this person better than other people in his or her field?
2. Choose two places that you know well (e.g., two cities, two schools, two gyms, or two restaurants). Compare the two places.
3. Have you ever tried to solve a problem and instead made the problem worse? What was the problem, what did you do, and how did that make the problem worse?
4. In most fields of study, researchers must evaluate competing theories. Briefly describe and compare two theories from your field of study.

Chapter 8
Gerunds and Infinitives

Introductory Focus

Gerunds and *infinitives* are two special English forms. A gerund is VERB + *-ing*. An infinitive is *to* + VERB. Although they are formed from verbs, gerunds and infinitives usually fill a noun's role in sentences, such as subject or object. They are sometimes called "the noun forms of a verb." Look at the following proverbs and sayings.

> Seeing is believing.
> Holding on to a hurt creates more hurt.
> Wisdom has two parts: (1) having a lot to say; (2) not saying it.
> To err is human; to forgive is divine.
> The devil finds work for idle hands to do.

Do you understand these sayings? Do you agree with them? Find the gerunds and infinitives. What do you notice about them?

Gerunds

Gerunds

In chapter 1, gerunds were called "names of activities." Gerunds are sometimes part of gerund phrases and are often used as subjects, complements, objects, or objects of prepositions. For simplicity, in this chapter the words *gerund phrase* refer to both single gerunds and longer gerund phrases.

Gerund phrases can be used as subjects.

Examples: <u>Eating</u> is a necessary part of life.
<u>Sky diving</u> is a dangerous sport.
<u>Walking in the moonlight</u> is romantic.
<u>Gaining insight into human behavior</u> is a major goal of psychology.
<u>Keeping precise records</u> is important in scientific experiments.

Gerund phrases are also used as complements.

Examples: The best part of our vacation was <u>sleeping in until noon each day.</u>
Tom's biggest goal in life is <u>accumulating personal wealth.</u>

Practice Exercise

Working with a partner or small group, list several possible gerund phrase subjects for each of the following predicates.

1. . . . is dangerous.

2. . . . is romantic.

3. . . . is expensive.

4. . . . is a waste of time.

5. . . . is fun.

Gerund phrases are also used as the objects of some verbs.[1]

Examples: I enjoy <u>swimming</u>.
Sue enjoys <u>walking in the rain</u>.
We postponed <u>making a decision</u>.
We anticipate <u>completing this project</u> next month.
The government delayed <u>providing tax relief for the private sector.</u>

The difficulty is that some verbs are followed by gerunds, some verbs are followed by infinitives, and some verbs are followed by neither. The reference charts on pages 113–14 list many of the common verbs in each category. No one has yet found a practical shortcut for memorizing which verbs belong in which category. When children grow up speaking English, they hear these forms so often that the gerunds and infinitives just "sound right" to them. Language learners have to practice saying and writing sentences with gerunds and infinitives until the correct forms just sound right to them too.

---

1. Such gerund phrases are sometimes called *gerund clauses* or *-ing clauses* and are considered a kind of clause without tense.

Practice Exercise

Working with a partner or small group, complete each of the following sentences with a gerund phrase.

1. I enjoy . . .

2. We usually avoid . . .

3. We anticipate . . .

4. The laws in this state prohibit . . .

5. A good teacher facilitates . . .

Gerund phrases are also used as objects of prepositions. If a verb comes after a preposition, the verb is always in its gerund form. (The only tricky point is that *to* is sometimes a preposition and sometimes part of an infinitive.)

Examples: Ann supplements her income by <u>tutoring math students</u> on weekends.
This store needs a strategy for <u>increasing sales to young adults</u>.
Gregor Mendel is credited with <u>discovering the principles of heredity</u>.
In Pat's life, the ratio of <u>sleeping</u> to <u>working</u> is quite high.
Learning vocabulary is an integral part of <u>learning a language</u>.

Practice Exercise

Working with a partner or small group, write sentences using the following VERB + PREPOSITION and ADJECTIVE + PREPOSITION combinations and a gerund phrase.

Example: be attributed to
Lung cancer is often attributed to smoking.

1. be involved in

2. can/can't conceive of

3. be capable of

4. be reluctant to

5. be crucial to

Gerund Forms

Gerund phrases can take several forms.

The negative form uses *not*.

Examples: I enjoy <u>not having any homework</u>.
           I dislike <u>not getting enough sleep</u>.

The passive form uses *being* + past participle.

Examples: Sue is afraid of <u>being bit by a dog</u>.
           <u>Being removed from his job</u> made Tom angry.

The perfect form uses *having* + past participle. These gerunds show that the activity happened before the time of the main verb in the sentence.

Examples: Pam appreciates <u>having received a good education</u>.
           Ron is sorry for <u>having hit his brother</u>.

Gerund phrases sometimes include a noun as subject of the gerund.

Examples: I don't like <u>him asking me questions</u>.
           Ann is tired of <u>Sue dominating their discussions</u>.

Older grammar books recommend using a possessive noun or pronoun before a gerund, but most speakers don't use possessive forms in gerund phrases.[2]

Examples: Do you mind <u>my smoking</u>? (good old-fashioned English)
Do you mind <u>me smoking</u>? (ordinary English)

The gerund forms can be combined. The gerund phrase in the following sentence is negative, perfect, and passive and includes a possessive pronoun subject.

Example: I am surprised at <u>his not having been given a scholarship</u>.

For Discussion and/or Writing

1. Have you ever been accused of or blamed for something that you didn't do? How did you handle the situation?
2. Very few people enjoy doing all of the necessary tasks in life. Are there any tasks that you hate, loathe, or detest doing? What are they? Which tasks do you enjoy, like, or welcome doing?

Infinitives

Infinitives

Infinitives (*to* + VERB) are often part of longer infinitive phrases. They are sometimes used as subjects and are frequently used as complements or objects of verbs. For simplicity, in this chapter the words *infinitive phrase* will refer to both simple infinitives and longer infinitive phrases.

Infinitives can be used as subjects.

Examples: <u>To vote</u> is an important civic duty.
<u>To provide good customer service</u> is our top priority.
<u>To serve customers quickly</u> is extremely important.

Although infinitive subjects are perfectly grammatical, English speakers rarely use them. In academic writing, however, authors sometimes use two infinitive phrases when they want to emphasize that you can't have one experience without having another experience at the same time (one experience is inherent in the other).

Examples: <u>To learn a second language</u> is <u>to learn a second culture</u>.
<u>To improve the welfare of our children</u> is <u>to improve the welfare of our nation</u>.

---

2. Biber et al., in *The Longman Grammar of Spoken and Written English,* report that in over 90 percent of cases, nouns and pronouns used before gerunds are not in possessive form.

Infinitive phrases are used as complements of linking verbs.

Examples: Our top priority is <u>to provide good customer service</u>.
               An important civic duty is <u>to vote</u>.
               Pam seems <u>to be happy</u>.
               This material seems <u>to retain heat well</u>.

Infinitive phrases are used as the objects of some verbs.[3]

Examples: We want <u>to feel safe</u>.
               The state plans <u>to initiate a new crime prevention program</u>.
               The government hopes <u>to reduce the incidence of crime</u>.

Again, the difficult part is learning which verbs take infinitives as objects. The reference charts on pages 113–14 may help, but more importantly, when you encounter a new verb, you should notice the words around it. When you study a verb, study the kinds of phrases that it is used with.

Practice Exercise

Working with a partner or small group, complete each of the following sentences with an infinitive phrase.

a. We need . . .

b. We are seeking . . .

c. On occasion, I have volunteered . . .

d. I expect . . .

e. Smart people decline . . .

3. Such infinitive phrases are sometimes called *infinitive clauses,* a kind of clause without tense.

Some verbs take infinitive objects in the pattern VERB + NOUN (or PRONOUN) + infinitive. The reference chart on page 113 includes several of these verbs.

Examples: I want <u>Tom to relax</u>.
I want <u>him to laugh at my jokes</u>.
The president convinced <u>the senate to support his policies</u>.
The president's words motivated <u>us to evaluate his policies carefully</u>.

Practice Exercise

Working with a partner or small group, complete each of the following sentences with an infinitive phrase.

a. Road signs often instruct us . . .

b. Money enables us . . .

c. The state licenses people . . .

d. We should select [name] . . .

e. I told you . . .

f. Nothing could induce me . . .

For Discussion and/or Writing

1. What are three things that you hope to do before you die? Why are these things important to you?

2. When you were a child, what did your parents and teachers expect you to do? What did they require you to do? What did they allow you to do on special occasions?

    Example: When I was eight years old, my parents expected me to clean my room and make my bed. They required me to go to bed at 9:00 P.M., but on New Year's Eve they allowed me to stay up until midnight.

    (If you are a parent, tell what you expect, require, and allow your child to do.)

3. Some people believe that the principal purpose of education is to equip students to earn a living. Others argue that education must also equip students to be informed citizens and leaders in a democracy. Still others say that an important purpose of education is to enable students to appreciate great works of music, literature, and visual art. What do you believe education should enable students to do?

Infinitive Forms

Like gerunds, infinitives can take several forms.

The negative form uses *not* or *never.* Traditionally, *not* and *never* go before *to,* but many speakers put them after *to.*

Examples: Tom expects <u>not to pass this class.</u>
                I urged Sue <u>never to waste time.</u>
                My plan is <u>to never buy a new car</u> again.

The passive form uses *to be* + past participle.

Examples: We all want <u>to be loved.</u>
                Lee expects <u>to be promoted</u> to a new job soon.

The progressive form uses *to be* + VERB + *-ing.*

Examples: Ann pretended <u>to be working</u> when her boss walked into the room.
                The storm appears <u>to be weakening.</u>

The perfect form uses *to have* + past participle. These infinitives show that the action happened prior to the time of the main verb.

Examples: We are pleased <u>to have completed the project</u> before the winter rains begin.
                It is better <u>to have loved</u> and lost than never <u>to have loved</u> at all. (a proverb)

The infinitive forms can be combined, although complex infinitive forms aren't needed very often.

Examples: Tom claims <u>to have been working</u> for the past three hours. (perfect, progressive infinitive)
It is sad <u>never to have been loved</u> by one's family. (negative, perfect, passive infinitive)

Practice Exercise

Accuracy practice: Compose sentences using the following words. Do not change the order of the words, but add words or change any word forms as necessary.

a. we / anticipate / complete / first phase / the project / next week

b. yesterday / Jon / finish / one job / and / proceed / start / another

c. Internet / facilitate / find / facts / quickly

d. driver of the car / acknowledge / exceed / speed limit

e. Dr. Nye / consent / speak on / theory / global warming

Infinitives as Complements

Some adjectives can be followed by an infinitive. The infinitive completes the meaning of the adjective.

Examples: Dr. Lee was <u>able to respond</u> to our request.
He was <u>happy to give</u> a lecture on U.S. immigration policy.
His lecture is <u>certain to stir</u> a reaction among students.

Infinitives are also used after certain adjectives in sentences with *it* as the subject. This pattern is frequently used in academic writing because it allows a writer to express an opinion without using *I* or *me*. Using this pattern helps give an objective tone to one's writing.

Examples: It is impossible <u>to prevent all international conflicts</u>.
It is very important <u>to resolve conflicts quickly</u>.
It is essential <u>to assess the potential risk of a conflict</u>.

Writers can make these sentences more specific by adding a phrase such as *for me* or *for her* before the infinitive.

Examples: It is hard <u>for me</u> to study in a noisy room.
It is impossible <u>for a color-blind person</u> to differentiate between red and green.
It is nearly impossible <u>for Tom</u> to keep a secret.

Practice Exercise

Working with a partner or small group, complete each of the following sentences with an infinitive phrase. Add *for me, for you,* et cetera, if you would like to.

a. It is easy . . .

b. It is hard . . .

c. It is good . . .

d. It is impossible . . .

e. It is vital . . .

Some nouns can also be followed by infinitives.

Examples: We have a problem to solve.
This is one way for us to illustrate the problem.
Our failure to generate enough revenue comes from our inability to write a good business plan.

Practice Exercise

Complete each of the following sentences with an infinitive phrase.

a. I recently made a decision . . .

b. I have no desire . . .

c. I need a place . . .

Infinitives of Purpose

Infinitives are often used to express purpose. In the following examples, the infinitive phrase tells the purpose of the action in the preceding clause.

Examples: I went to the store <u>to buy milk</u>.
Pat uses a hearing aid <u>to compensate for his deafness</u>.
The government imposed a curfew <u>to restore quiet in the streets</u>.

Infinitives of purpose may begin with *in order to,* but this phrase is often shortened to just *to.*

Long Form	Short Form
I went to the store in order to buy milk. We used a formula in order to convert pounds to kilograms.	I went to the store to buy milk. We used a formula to convert pounds to kilograms.

An infinitive of purpose can also be placed before a clause.

Examples: (In order) to secure adequate revenue for schools, the state must raise taxes.
To demonstrate her commitment to education, the governor visited several schools yesterday.
To attain a college degree, a student must work hard for several years.

Never use *for* + VERB to express a purpose. Always use *to* + VERB.

NOT ENGLISH   I go to school for study English.

For Discussion and/or Writing

1. What can other students do to assist you in improving your English skills? What can you do to assist others?
2. What do you usually do to occupy your time while you are waiting in lines, waiting for an appointment, or waiting "on hold" on the telephone?
3. Have you ever undertaken a self-improvement project? What did you decide to do? Was it easy or difficult to attain your goals?
4. It is often wise to conform to social norms in dress and manners. Sometimes, however, social pressure is used to enforce a rigid conformity that limits freedom and creativity. Choose one aspect of community life in which conformity is an issue and state your opinion. For example, should elementary and high school students be required to follow a dress code or to wear uniforms? Should business employees be expected to wear suits or other formal clothing? Should employees be allowed to dye their hair unusual colors, to have tattoos, or to wear nose rings? Are young people ultimately happier if their parents allow them to make most decisions for themselves or if their parents teach them to follow the community customs?

Trouble Spots and Tricky Points

1. A few verbs are used with either a gerund or an infinitive, depending on the meaning the speaker wants to express.

Stop
Stop + gerund = stop an activity; *stop* + infinitive = stop for a purpose. Therefore, the following long sentence has two short forms.

> Long form: I stopped driving my car in order to eat lunch.
> Short form: I stopped driving. (I stopped an activity—driving.)
> Short form: I stopped to eat. (I stopped for a purpose—to eat.)

Remember
Remember + gerund = think about a past activity.

Examples: I remember playing with my friends when I was a child.
I remember climbing trees, building forts, and sewing clothes for our dolls.

Remember + infinitive = not forget to do something.

Examples: I remembered to bring my book to class.
I must remember to pay my rent tomorrow.
Lee never remembers to turn off his cell phone before class starts.

Regret

Regret + gerund = feel bad about doing something.

Examples: I regret wasting time yesterday.
Sue regrets not taking math last semester.

Regret + infinitive = announcement of bad news.

Examples: Theta Airlines regrets to announce that today's flight will be two hours late.
I regret to say that no one passed the English test yesterday.

Try

Try + infinitive = attempt to achieve a goal.

Examples: I will try to call you tonight.
The government tried to suppress all forms of protest.
Lee tries to look cheerful at all times.

Try + gerund = attempt to solve a problem by an action.

Example: My houseplants are not growing well. I tried giving them water, but they remained small and unhealthy. I tried giving them fertilizer, but they remained small and unhealthy. Next, I will try moving them into a place with better light. (These activities—giving water, giving fertilizer, moving the plants—are experiments. If one action doesn't solve the problem, I will try doing something else.)

2. A few ADJECTIVE + infinitive combinations have an unusual pattern of meaning. Most adjectives that are used with infinitives follow the same pattern of meaning as the adjective *happy*.

Examples: Pat is happy to read this book. (Pat is happy for Pat to read this book.)
Ann is reluctant to quit working. (Ann is reluctant for Ann to quit working.)
Jon is eager to please. (Jon is eager for Jon to please other people.)

A few adjectives have a different meaning pattern.

Examples: Jon is easy to please. (It is easy for other people to please Jon.)
This book is difficult to read. (It is difficult for people to read this book.)

Some adjectives in this group include

easy	possible	fun	important	safe
difficult	impossible	interesting	nice	dangerous
hard	challenging	boring		

Language learners sometimes make mistakes with adjectives in this group.

NOT ENGLISH   I am easy to read this book.
Ron is difficult to sleep.

ENGLISH   It is easy for me to read this book.
It is hard for Ron to sleep.

REFERENCE CHART
Some Verbs That Pattern VERB + Infinitive

Example: We agreed to do the work.

agree	choose	decline	intend	plan	seek	wait
appear	claim	deserve	learn	prefer*	seem	want
ask	commence*	expect	like*	pretend	start*	
attempt	consent	guarantee	love*	proceed	tend	
begin*	continue*	hate*	need	promise	undertake	
cease*	decide	hope	offer	resolve	volunteer	

* These verbs can also be followed by a gerund.

REFERENCE CHART
Some Verbs That Pattern VERB + (PRO)NOUN + Infinitive

Example: We advised him to do the work.

advise*	challenge	equip	intend	persuade	tell
allow	commission	expect	license	promise	urge
ask	compel	force	like*	provoke	want
assign	convince	guarantee	motivate	require*	
assist	design	incline	need	select	
authorize*	dispose	induce	oblige	stimulate	
cause	enable	instruct	permit*	teach	

* These verbs can also be followed by a gerund.

REFERENCE CHART
Some Verbs That Pattern VERB + Gerund

Example: They acknowledged doing poor work.

acknowledge	commence*	enjoy	like*	require
admit	consider	face	loathe	start*
advise	contemplate	facilitate	love*	stress
anticipate	continue*	forgo	mind	tolerate
appreciate	delay	hate*	necessitate	visualize
authorize	deny	imply	permit	welcome
begin	detest	involve	postpone	
can't stand*	eliminate	justify	predict	
cease*	emphasize	keep (on)	prefer	

*These verbs can also be followed by an infinitive.

Make, Let, and Have

The three verbs *make, let,* and *have* follow a special pattern. American English speakers usually use *help* in this same pattern.

Sentence	Meaning
Tom made Dan wash the car.	Tom used pressure. Dan didn't really want to wash the car.
Tom had Dan repair the car.	Tom assigned the repair job to Dan, or Tom paid Dan to repair the car.
Tom let Dan drive the car.	Tom allowed Dan to drive the car.
Tom helped Dan wax the car.	Tom assisted Dan in waxing the car.

Notice:

1. *Make* is somewhat strong and implies that some force or pressure was used.
2. *Have* is used when one person has a right to make requests of or assign tasks to another person.
3. *Let* is used when one person permits or allows another person to do something.
4. *Help* is used when one person aids another. It is also correct to say, "Tom helped Dan to wax the car."

Examples: The bad weather made us go indoors.
Our teachers made us study classical Greek literature, and
eventually we learned to like it.
Dr. Nye had Dr. Dun explain his theories to all the professors in
the department.
The math professor had students incorporate statistics into their
papers.
The teacher let the students leave class early.
Her English professor let Pam submit her paper two days late.
Ann helped Ron choose a topic for his paper.
His writing instructor helped Ron revise the first draft of his
paper.

Practice Exercises

1. What are some things that make you laugh? What are some things that
    make you cry? Write at least three complete sentences.

    Examples: Beautiful weddings always make me cry.
    Hearing a baby laugh makes me laugh too.

2. Think of your current (or past) job. Make a list of three things that your
    supervisor often has (or had) you do. If you have never had a job, list three
    things that parents or teachers often have you do.

3. A slogan from a famous public service advertising campaign in the United
    States is, "Friends don't let friends drive drunk." It means that a true
    friend will never let a person drive a car after the person has been
    drinking alcohol. Make a list of five things that a good friend will let or
    not let a person do.

Chapter 9

Parallel Structure

Introductory Focus

Parallel structure occurs when phrases, clauses, or complete sentences follow the same grammar pattern while using different words and expressing different ideas. Notice the grammar patterns in the following two proverbs.

> Kindness is a language that the deaf can hear, the blind can see, and the mute can speak.
> Early to bed and early to rise makes a man healthy, wealthy, and wise.

Do you agree with the ideas in these proverbs? Do you notice any repetition of grammar patterns in these proverbs?

Using Parallel Structure

Using parallel structure is a way to make your writing beautiful. In truth, parallel structure is more a matter of style than a question of grammar, and because it requires planning and editing, parallel structure is more frequent in formal speeches and writing than in conversation. When the preceding proverbs are rewritten without parallel structure, the meaning is clear, but the sentences are ugly.

> Kindness is a language that people who are deaf can hear, that blind people are able to see, and that even people who don't talk out loud know how to speak.
> To have an early bedtime and then get up early is a way for a man to become healthy, get a lot of money, and be a wise person.

When you join phrases or clauses with a conjunction, try to use the same grammar pattern in each of the phrases or clauses. Here are some examples.

Ugly   I like to swim, going to movies, and to read.

Better   I like to swim, go to movies, and read.

I like to swim, to go to movies, and to read.

I like swimming, going to movies, and reading.

Ugly   Bob traveled to New York via Chicago, and then he flew to the city of London, and finally he went to Paris.

Better   Bob traveled to Paris via Chicago, New York, and London.

OK   The company began in 1923, but it had to temporarily stop production during World War II, and then finally, in 1998, the owners decided to close the business.

Better   The company commenced operations in 1923, suspended production during World War II, and permanently ceased operations in 1998.

Practice Exercises

1. Use parallel structure to improve the following sentences.

   a. The temperature here fluctuates between a low of 35°F and the highest temperature, which is 95°F.

   b. The duration of treatment for this type of injury ranges between six weeks and half of a year.

   c. Sue doesn't give her children foods that are processed, refined, or have a coating of sugar on them.

   d. Tom's profits from running his business were offset by losses from the stocks that he sold.

e. This skin cream will heal acne, prevent you from getting sunburned, and reverse the effects of aging.

f. Babies explore their environment by manipulating objects and put the objects in their mouths.

2. Choose something you have already written. Look through it and try to find places where you can make it more beautiful by creating parallel structure.

For Discussion and/or Writing

1. Create a list of instructions for a simple task, such as cooking eggs or changing a lightbulb. Make sure the items on the list are in parallel structure.
2. Do you think watching television is a waste of time? What are some of the benefits of and some of the problems with watching television? Try to use parallel structures in your response.

Chapter 10
Subordination and Transition: Adverb Clauses

Introductory Focus

As an advanced learner of English, you already know and use several *subordinating conjunctions*[1] (such as *because* and *when*), *transitional words*[2] (such as *however*), and *transitional phrases* (such as *first of all* and *in conclusion*); you can, however, improve your writing style by increasing the variety of conjunctions and phrases that you use. Notice the structure of the following sayings.

> When you are arguing with an idiot, make sure the other person isn't doing the same thing.
> Dig the well before you are thirsty.
> When you are born, you are crying and everyone around you is smiling. Live so that when you die, you are smiling and everyone around you is crying.
> All the so-called "secrets of success" won't work unless you do.
> An error doesn't become a mistake until you choose to ignore it.

Do you understand these sentences? Do you agree with them? How many clauses are there in each sentence? Where does each clause begin and end?

In good English writing, it is the writer's job to make the relationship between ideas very clear. As a general rule, English writing is considered more effective, beautiful, and sophisticated if the writer puts some of the information in dependent clauses and uses subordinating conjunctions and transitional words and phrases to show the relationship between ideas.

---

1. Some grammar books call these *subordinators*.

2. Some grammar books call these *linking adverbials* or *conjunctive adverbs*.

Independent Clauses	Connected Ideas
Tom is developing regulations for protecting a species of fish. Sue is computing the cost of implementing the regulations.	While Tom is developing regulations for protecting a species of fish, Sue is computing the cost of implementing them. Tom is developing regulations for protecting a species of fish. At the same time, Sue is computing the cost of implementing them.

Notice:

1. In the two sentences that show connected ideas, the word *while* and the phrase *at the same time* have approximately the same meaning, but the sentences have different grammatical structures.
2. *While* is a subordinating conjunction and introduces a dependent clause.
3. *At the same time* is a transitional expression and introduces an independent sentence.
4. As you learn to connect ideas, you must learn which words and expressions create dependent clauses and which words and expressions belong to independent sentences. The reference chart on pages 122–23 will help.

The preference for using subordinating conjunctions and transitional words and phrases is only a general rule. In many cases, simple sentences are appropriate. As you read textbooks, magazines, et cetera, notice the ways authors connect their ideas. For example, engineers tend to use a different group of expressions than historians use. You can learn to sound more like an engineer, a historian, or a member of any other profession by studying writing in a particular field.

Although there are many subordinating conjunctions and transitional expressions in English, this chapter concentrates on those that cause trouble for many writers and those that are usually used only in academic writing.

Ways to Connect Ideas

There are four basic ways to show a connection of ideas.

You can join two independent clauses with a semicolon.

Independent Clauses	Connected Clauses
Commodities such as wheat, cotton, and steel can be transported by railroad or by truck. Transportation companies compete for this business.	Commodities such as wheat, cotton, and steel can be transported by railroad or by truck; transportation companies compete for this business.

Notice: The semicolon tells the reader that there is a connection between the ideas of the two clauses, but it doesn't explain the connection. This is not a very popular way to connect ideas.

You can join two clauses with a conjunction—*and, but, or,* or *nor.*

Independent Clauses	Connected Clauses
Sales in overseas markets are declining. Sales in domestic markets are stable.	Sales in overseas markets are declining, but sales in domestic markets are stable.

Notice:
1. There is usually a comma before the conjunction. Some writers omit the comma if the clauses are short.
2. Some writers begin sentences with a conjunction. This is a conversational style of writing.

You can join two clauses with a subordinating conjunction.

Independent Clauses	Connected Clauses
Agriculture provides 80 percent of the jobs here. Our local economy is heavily reliant on farming.	Because agriculture provides 80 percent of the jobs here, our local economy is heavily reliant on farming.
Most of the money from this fund-raising event will help sick children. A portion of the proceeds will go to support research.	Although most of the money from this fund-raising event will help sick children, a portion of the proceeds will go to support research.

Notice:
1. A subordinating conjunction (such as *because* or *although*) begins a dependent clause. In writing, a dependent clause never stands alone.
2. The dependent clause may come before or after the independent clause.
3. If the dependent clause comes before the independent clause, separate the clauses with a comma.

You can use a transitional word or phrase.

Independent Ideas	Connected Ideas
Several companies are constructing new earthquake-safe buildings. State engineers are reinforcing old buildings and bridges.	Several companies are constructing new, earthquake-safe buildings. At the same time, state engineers are reinforcing old buildings and bridges.
A body temperature of 98.6°F is normal. A temperature of 100°F or higher is a symptom of disease.	A body temperature of 98.6°F is normal. A temperature of 100°F or higher, however, is a symptom of disease.

Notice:
1. Transitional words and phrases are part of independent sentences.
2. Transitional words and phrases can come at the beginning, middle, or end of a sentence. Use commas to separate them from the rest of the sentence.

REFERENCE CHART
Subordinating Conjunctions and Transitional Expressions

Use	Subordinating Conjunctions	Transitional Expressions
Cause	because, as, since, as long as, so long as, whereas	for this reason, on this account
Purpose	so, so that, in order that, in the hope that	for this purpose, with this intention, to this end
Result	so	therefore, thus, consequently, as a consequence, as a result, hence

Use	Subordinating Conjunctions	Transitional Expressions
Condition (See chapter 13.)	if, even if, unless	otherwise, under other circumstances
Manner		likewise, similarly, in a similar way, in much the same way
Addition		furthermore, moreover, additionally, in addition, also, further
To add an example		for example, for instance, as an example, to illustrate
To list or expand		to enumerate, to elaborate
Conclusion or summary		to conclude, in conclusion, finally, in summary, to sum up, to summarize, in sum, in brief, all in all
Contrast	while, whereas	in contrast, on the one hand . . . on the other hand, on the contrary, conversely
Contrast or concession	although, though, even though, while, albeit, granted that	however, granted, nevertheless, nonetheless, even so
To repeat		in other words, to clarify
To suggest a substitute idea		instead, rather, alternatively
Sequence	before, while, after, since, ever since	then, next, later, subsequently, first, firstly, second, secondly, last, finally, simultaneously

Practice Exercise

Correct the punctuation mistakes in the following sentences.

a. Ron is unhappy in his new school. Because he doesn't adapt well to new situations.

b. Cactus plants are adapted to dry climates, therefore, they survive in deserts.

c. Jan attaches labels to all of her computer disks. So that she doesn't lose them.

d. Ann sent an attachment with her e-mail, however, Tom didn't know how to open it.

e. Sue is emotionally attached to her old toys, consequently, she doesn't want to give them away.

Troublesome Subordinating Conjunctions

As long as, so long as

As long as and *so long as* are used in two ways.

They usually have a meaning similar to *if*.

Examples: We can finish painting the house so long as it doesn't rain.
You won't need to pay a late fee as long as you register before 5:00 P.M. today.
The bank does not charge fees for money transfers as long as you keep your deposit balance above $1,000.

In some casual conversational situations, *as long as* and *so long as* have a meaning similar to *because*.

Examples: If Sue and Ann are watching TV and Sue gets up for any reason, she might say, "As long as I'm up, can I get you something from the kitchen?"
If Sue decides to go to the store, Ann might say, "As long as you're going to the store anyway, could you please buy me a newspaper? I'll give you the money."

Unless

Unless means approximately "if not" or "if this doesn't happen." It is used to introduce a statement telling what event will change a plan or what event will prevent a prediction from coming true.

Examples: We will have a picnic unless it rains. (We will have a picnic if it doesn't rain.)
Unless she is sick, Sue comes to class. (If she is not sick, Sue comes to class.)
Our city can't construct more roads unless the state legislature provides financing. (The city is unable to construct more roads. This situation will change if the legislature gives the city some money.)
I'm going to eat the last piece of cake unless you tell me not to. (I plan to eat the last piece of cake. I will change my plan if you tell me not to eat it.)

Notice: In the first example sentence, the speakers plan on having a picnic; only one thing can stop the picnic (rain). The second example sentence identifies Sue as a very faithful student; only one thing can stop her from coming to class (sickness).

Even if

Even if has approximately the same meaning as *if* but carries emphasis. *Even if* communicates that if the situation changes, the statement of the main clause will remain true.

Examples: Nothing can stop me from coming to class tomorrow. Even if I am sick, I will come to class. Even if there is an earthquake, I will come to class. Even if there is a hurricane, a volcanic eruption, and a tornado, I will come to class.
Delta Corporation does not expect to show a profit this year, even if the economy improves in the next six months. Income will be less than expenses even if sales increase by 15 percent.

Even though

Even though has approximately the same meaning as *though* or *although* but carries emphasis.

Examples: Although I had many reasons not to come to class today, I came to class. Even though I have a headache, I came to class. Even though I have not finished my homework, I came to class. Even though the weather is terrible, my favorite team is playing on television, and my sick mother needs me at home, I came to class. Even though the Sigma Corporation has developed some very innovative new technology, it has not received much publicity. Even though the test was very fair, many students were unhappy with the outcome.

While

While has two meanings.

The first and basic meaning is "at the same time."

Examples: Lee was practicing the piano while Pat was trying to study.
              While Tom cooked dinner, Sue watched TV.

The second meaning of *while* is similar to *although*. It signals a contrast.

Examples: Milk is very nutritious, while coffee is low in nutrients.
              While Lee is an adult, Sue is still an adolescent.
              While an adult male pheasant is a very colorful bird, an adult female pheasant is usually brown.

Sometimes the two meanings—"at the same time" and "in contrast"—overlap.

Example: While people in rural areas of Russia were starving, aristocrats in St. Petersburg were building increasingly elaborate palaces.

Whereas

Whereas is used in formal writing but is rare in conversation. It has two meanings.

In very formal government documents, *whereas* means *because*.

Example: Whereas the leading cause of death among young people ages 15 to 24 in the U.S. is alcohol-related car crashes, and whereas alcohol use also is associated with homicides, suicides, and drownings, the other three leading causes of death among youth, now, therefore, I, Pat Lee, mayor of the city of Lewistown, urge all who reside in this city to support the American Academy of Pediatrics in its efforts to prevent underage drinking.

In other writing, *whereas* introduces a strong contrast.

Examples: Whereas Ernest Hemingway wrote with very short sentences, John Steinbeck often used very long ones.
Hemingway wrote with very short sentences, whereas Steinbeck often used very long ones.
The population density of Singapore is high, whereas the population density of Canada is quite low.

Notice:
1. *Whereas* begins a dependent clause.
2. *Whereas* may be used to mark either half of a contrast.
3. The clauses in a sentence using *whereas* are separated by a comma.

Albeit

Albeit is used in academic writing but is rare in conversation. The word comes from Middle English *al be it,* which meant "although it is true that," and it signals a concession. (See page 130 for more information on concession.)

Examples: Nuclear power production continues in Ukraine, albeit the worst nuclear power accident in history happened here.
Albeit Ukraine is economically depressed, it has rich natural resources.

Practice Exercise

Complete the following sentences in ways that make good sense.

a. I will come to class tomorrow unless . . .

b. Unless Ann is sick or injured, she . . .

c. Ron won't reveal our secret, even if . . .

d. Ken demonstrates many fine character qualities, whereas Ron . . .

e. Whereas Pam's friends think she is a saint, Sue's friends . . .

f. Even though Professor Lee usually explains ideas in simple terminology, . . .

g. Jan is watching television, even though . . .

h. As long as you lock your car, no one . . .

i. Pat's job is only temporary, while Sue's job . . .

Troublesome Transitional Expressions

Subsequently, Consequently

Subsequently is similar in meaning to *later.*

Example:	In 1999, the city leaders thought about building a new library. Subsequently, in 2001, they abandoned the idea.

Consequently and *as a consequence* are similar in meaning to *therefore.* They signal a result.

Example:	The city leaders want to build a new library. Consequently, they must raise taxes.

Hence

Hence signals a result. It can be used at the beginning or middle of a clause, but not at the end. It is used in academic writing and is rare in conversation.

Examples:	In the U.S., military service is voluntary. Hence, the army advertises on television. In some countries, military service is compulsory. There are, hence, no TV advertisements for the military in those countries.

Moreover, Furthermore, in Addition

Moreover, furthermore, and *in addition* are similar in meaning to *and.* They are used in academic writing to introduce added information or additional arguments.

Example: A starfish needs water in order to function normally. Furthermore, if it is not kept moist, it will quickly die.

For Example, For Instance

The phrases *for example* and *for instance* are synonyms, are used in academic writing, and don't appear often in other kinds of writing.

Example: Don't mix metaphors when you write. For instance, don't say that your enemy is a chicken who hides behind his mother's skirts.

To Enumerate, To Elaborate

To enumerate introduces a numbered list.

Example: There are many reasons not to smoke. To enumerate: first, smoking harms one's heart; second, smoking is bad for one's lungs; third, smoking costs a lot.

To elaborate introduces more details on a subject.

Example: Smoking is bad for one's lungs. To elaborate, smoking increases the odds of getting asthma, emphysema, or lung cancer.

In Contrast

In contrast indicates that two things are quite different.

Examples: Earth's atmosphere is about 20 percent oxygen. In contrast, Mars's atmosphere has almost no oxygen.
In contrast to Earth's atmosphere, the atmosphere on Mars has almost no oxygen.
Lee is a man of high integrity. In contrast, his son Bob lies, cheats, and steals.

On the One Hand . . . on the Other Hand

On the one hand . . . on the other hand is used to emphasize strong contrasts and counterarguments.[3] Don't use *on the other hand* as a simple synonym for *but*; *on the other hand* is stronger than *but*.

Example:　On the one hand, television allows us to see and hear some of the greatest musical performances in the world. On the other hand, it also brings into our homes some of the silliest and most trivial music ever written.

Conversely

Conversely is used when one situation is the exact opposite of another.

Example:　When prices go down, sales increase. Conversely, when prices go up, sales decline.

On the Contrary

On the contrary has a very specific use. You should use it only when you are emphatically rejecting an idea and want to say that the opposite is true.

Examples:　Sue is not poor. On the contrary, she is very rich.
Tom is not weak. On the contrary, he is a champion weight lifter.

Sue: Is Pam a good cook?
Tom: Certainly not! On the contrary, she burns nearly everything she prepares.

Kim: I think O'Hare is a small airport near Chicago.
Lee: On the contrary, it is one of the busiest airports in the U.S.

Granted, Nevertheless, Nonetheless, Even So

Granted, nevertheless, nonetheless, and *even so* are all phrases of concession for academic writing. If you concede an idea, you agree that the idea is true, but you say that another idea is even more important. This is the "yes, but" pattern. *Granted* functions like *yes. Nonetheless, nevertheless,* and *even so* function like *but*.

Examples:　Yes, Seattle is a very gray, rainy city, but I love living here.
Seattle is a very gray, rainy city. Nevertheless, I love living here.
Granted, Seattle is a very gray, rainy city. I love living here anyway.

---

3. Some writers believe that *on the other hand* should not be used unless it follows *on the one hand*.

Instead, Rather, Alternatively

Instead, rather, and *alternatively* are used to introduce a substitute idea or choice. *Instead* and *rather* usually mean, "this, not that." *Alternatively* usually means, "this or that."

Examples: We shouldn't show bias against some ethnic groups. Rather, we should treat all people equally.
Ron didn't confer with other people about his decision. Instead, he made the decision alone and without getting anyone's advice.
We could raise the price of lunch at our restaurant. Alternatively, we could substitute cheap ingredients for the expensive ones in our recipes.

A Few More Troublesome Expressions

Thereby, Whereby, and Hereby

The word *whereby* appears in academic writing but is very rare in other kinds of English. It means "by this" or "through this," and it creates a subordinate clause.

Examples: Ron invented a device whereby he was able to heat his home at very little cost.
The Lambda Corporation has an incentive plan whereby workers receive extra money when they increase the company's sales.

The word *thereby* is very similar to *whereby,* but *thereby* is part of an independent clause.

Examples: Ann bought 40,000 shares of stock in the Lambda Corporation. She thereby became a major owner of the company.
Sue violated several company regulations and, thereby, lost her job.

The word *hereby* is very rarely used. It means "by this" and is usually used only in very formal official documents.

Notwithstanding and Despite

The words *despite* and *notwithstanding* are prepositions meaning "in spite of." They are used with noun phrases, not clauses, and signal a contrast or concession. The word *notwithstanding* is used in formal writing and is an unusual preposition because it may either precede or follow a noun phrase.

Examples: Despite the big smile on his face, internally Tom felt worried and sad.

Tom continued to smile despite his problems.

Notwithstanding protests from environmental activists, the president today convened a meeting of the U.S. Energy Commission to discuss allowing greater use of Alaskan oil reserves.

Environmental issues notwithstanding, many industry leaders argue that we must increase output from oil fields within the U.S.

Using Transitional Expressions to Organize an Essay

Very frequently, academic writing is organized around a *thesis.*

A thesis is a sentence.	A noun phrase states a topic, but a *thesis* must have a subject and a verb.
A thesis answers a question.	If a thesis answers an interesting question, it is probably an interesting thesis and may lead to an interesting paper.
A thesis can be debated.	A thesis doesn't need to be highly controversial, but it should be something that could cause intelligent, well-informed people to say: "Are you sure of that? Why do you think that is true?"

The brief essays in the following practice exercises follow the classic pattern for presenting an argument in English. First, there is an introduction that states a thesis. Next, the writer discusses arguments against the thesis and either refutes or concedes them. Then, the writer presents additional arguments in favor of the thesis. Last, the writer summarizes the argument and restates the thesis. Transitional expressions can be used to help the reader follow this outline. Using transitional expressions helps give the essay *coherence.* That means the essay "sticks together" well.

Practice Exercises

1. Underline the transitional words and expressions in the following, brief essay. Notice the function of each one, indicated at the right margin.

In the history of the world, several languages have been used for international communication, but there has never before been one language that could be used all around the world. Today, English is becoming a global language because of economic factors.	(thesis)
Some people say that English isn't spoken widely enough to be called a global language. Granted, the majority of people in the world don't speak English. Even so, English is spoken all around the world. Other people think that English has become a global language because it has a simple grammar and a large vocabulary. Linguists disagree. They tell us that all languages are complex and that all languages can express any idea.	concession refutation
There are three main reasons English is becoming a global language. First, historically, the economic power of English-speaking nations spread English around the world. In the 18th and 19th centuries, Britain established colonies in many parts of the world. Then, in the 20th century, the military and economic power of the United States ensured the widespread use of English. As a result, English is spoken on every continent on the globe.	sequence sequence result
Second, many people believe that they can get better jobs if they learn English, both because most international business is conducted in English and because many multinational corporations use English as their language of internal communication. For many people, learning English has become an important step toward professional advancement.	sequence cause
Lastly, English is used for a large part of Internet communication. Approximately 80 percent of Web pages are in English. Consequently, people want to learn English so they can find information on the Web.	sequence result
In brief, many factors are influencing the spread of English. Economic forces of the past (colonies and trade), present (international business), and future (widespread use of the Internet) are making English a global language.	summary (thesis)

2. Fill each blank in the following brief essay with a suitable word or phrase from this list: *because, finally, first, for example, for instance, in conclusion, nevertheless, nonetheless, in contrast, secondly, therefore, third, to summarize, unless.* Use each expression in the list only once. You will not need to use every expression in the list.

Many families own pets. Pets provide comfort and companionship, and one of the most enjoyable pets is a cat. In

fact, _____ cats have many fine qualities, every family | cause
should think about acquiring a cat.

Granted, cats are not perfect. Cats have propensities toward killing songbirds and bringing dead mice into the house. | concession and contrast

_____, there are many good reasons to own a cat.

_____, cats are simple to care for. _____, | sequence
cats keep themselves clean. One very rarely has to bathe a cat. | example

Dogs, _____, develop foul odors if they aren't bathed | contrast
regularly.

_____, cats don't make a lot of noise _____ | sequence condition example
they are in danger. _____, if a dog attacks a cat, the cat
may yowl. Likewise, if a person steps on a cat's tail, the cat may
hiss quite loudly.

_____, cats are pleasurable to watch. Ever since | sequence
cats were domesticated by the ancient Egyptians, people have
admired cats' aristocratic good looks and graceful movements.

_____, cats are easy to care for, quiet, and | conclusion

beautiful. _____, everyone should consider owning a | result
cat.

For Discussion and/or Writing

1. Where do you think is the best place in the world for a vacation?
2. Which approach to resolving interpersonal conflicts do you think is usually better, direct verbal confrontation or indirect methods, such as communicating through a mutual friend?

3. Do you think all students should be required to take music and art classes?
4. Government subsidies are often controversial. Do you think it is appropriate for governments to tax citizens in order to provide subsidies for artists, for small businesses that are just getting started, or for large corporations that provide many jobs? Pick one area and explain why you think subsidies in the area are or are not appropriate.

Chapter 11
Adjective Clauses

Introductory Focus

All languages have ways of giving specific information about a noun by using words (adjectives), phrases, and clauses. These words, phrases, and clauses *modify* the noun. Look at the following proverbs.

> People who live in glass houses shouldn't throw stones.
> A person who gossips to you will gossip about you.
> He who angers you controls you.
> A child's life is like a piece of paper on which every person leaves a mark.
> The hand that rocks the cradle rules the world.
> The heart that loves is always young.

Do you know any of these sayings? Do you agree with them? How many clauses are there in each proverb? Where are the subjects? Where are the verbs?

The dependent clauses in the preceding proverbs are sometimes called *adjective clauses,* because they modify nouns, and are sometimes called *relative clauses.* This chapter uses the term *adjective clause.* All languages have ways of creating adjective clauses, but the rules are very different in different languages.[1] Many people have trouble correctly producing adjective clauses, even if they understand English well. In written work especially, if adjective clauses are not correctly produced, readers may have great difficulty in understanding what the writer meant to say.

---

1. You may find it helpful to think about the languages you speak and consciously notice the differences between adjective clauses in English and adjective clauses in other languages.

Definition of Terms

In adjective clauses, the words *who, whom, which,* and *that* are called *relative pronouns.*

Using adjective clauses is a way to combine two sentences. In each of the following examples, the second sentence becomes an adjective clause.

A *subject adjective clause* involves a change in the subject of the second sentence.

Example: Here is a child. The child likes tomatoes.
Here is a child <u>who likes tomatoes</u>.

An *object adjective clause* involves a change in the direct object of the second sentence.

Example: Here is a child. Everyone likes the child.
Here is a child <u>that everyone likes</u>.

A *preposition adjective clause* involves a change in the object of a preposition in the second sentence.

Example: Here is a child. We talked to the child.
Here is a child <u>that we talked to</u>.

Subject Adjective Clauses

For most people, the easiest adjective clauses to master are subject adjective clauses. In these clauses, the relative pronoun in the adjective clause is the subject of the adjective clause.

Two Sentences	One Sentence with an Adjective Clause
The conference had a program. The program was quite varied.	The conference had a <u>program</u> that was quite varied. ↑ (program)
The conference featured a speaker. The speaker studies storms.	The conference featured a <u>speaker</u> who studies storms. ↑ (speaker)
Storms are dangerous. Storms damage power lines.	<u>Storms</u> that damage power lines are dangerous. ↑ (storms)

Notice:

1. *Who* and *that* may be used for people; *which* and *that* may be used for things.
2. For people, writers usually use *who,* but speakers very often use *that.*
3. The verb in the adjective clause is singular if the noun that the clause modifies is singular.
4. English has a very strong rule that says every clause must have a subject. Therefore, relative pronouns can never be omitted from subject adjective clauses in Standard English.

NOT ENGLISH	I know a man owns a boat.
	There was an accident happened.
ENGLISH	I know a man who owns a boat.
	There was an accident. OR
	An accident happened.

Practice Exercises

1. Rewrite each of the following sentences, making a subject adjective clause from the clause in parentheses.

   Example: Last year, Alaska experienced an earthquake (the earthquake exceeded 7.0 on the Richter scale).
   Last year, Alaska experienced an earthquake that exceeded 7.0 on the Richter scale.

   a. Lee bought an insurance policy (the policy covers earthquake damage to his home).

   b. The graph (the graph shows how much the policy will pay) is on page 3.

   c. An earthquake (the earthquake measures 6.0 on the Richter scale) is capable of causing serious structural damage to buildings.

d. The insurance agent (the insurance agent sold Lee the policy) said that many people are buying these policies.

e. Scientists (the scientists study earthquakes) predict that Seattle will experience a very severe earthquake in the future.

2. Write a subject adjective clause to describe the underlined word in each of the following sentences.

Example: I remember the <u>earthquake</u>.
I remember the earthquake that happened in 1998.

a. The <u>professor</u> will discuss earthquakes in deep layers of rock.

b. There was an <u>earthquake</u>.

c. Many <u>buildings</u> sustained minor damage.

d. Sue called home to reassure her <u>mother</u>.

e. The <u>people</u> will file claims with their insurance companies.

Object Adjective Clauses

Many people find object adjective clauses a little harder to use at first than subject adjective clauses. In object adjective clauses, the relative pronoun in the adjective clause is the object of the verb in the adjective clause.

Two Sentences	One Sentence with an Adjective Clause
Sue knows the man. We met the man yesterday.	Sue knows the <u>man</u> whom we met yesterday. ↑ (man)
The data came from reliable sources. We used the data.	The <u>data</u> that we used came from reliable sources. ↑ (data)
Ten scholars contributed to the report. We published the report.	Ten scholars contributed to the <u>report</u> that we published. ↑ (report)

Notice:
1. *Who, whom,* and *that* may be used for persons; *which* and *that* may be used for things.
2. In very formal writing, *whom,* not *who,* is used in this structure.
3. The relative pronoun may be omitted from an object adjective clause, because the pronoun isn't a subject.

   Examples: Sue knows the man we met yesterday.
   The data we used came from reliable sources.
   Ten scholars contributed to the report we published.

4. Unlike many languages, English doesn't allow a second pronoun in a sentence with an object adjective clause.[2]

   NOT ENGLISH   The book that I read it was interesting.
   Tom gave the book to the teacher who he likes her.

Practice Exercises

1. Rewrite each of the following sentences, making an object adjective clause from the clause in parentheses.

Example: Pam devoted a lot of time to the class (she taught the class).
   Pam devoted a lot of time to the class that she taught.

---

2. This pronoun is usually called a *resumptive pronoun.* In speech, especially if a sentence is long and complicated, you may hear people violate the rule against such pronouns in English. This is usually a sign that the speaker is having trouble organizing his or her thoughts (e.g., "I have a friend who is an artist and who she paints pictures."). Using resumptive pronouns is not acceptable in writing.

    a. Pam edited the report (Tim wrote the report).

    b. The concern (people feel the concern) about earthquakes is legitimate.

    c. Information (scientists obtained the information from studying previous earthquakes) suggests that Seattle is very vulnerable to earthquakes.

    d. Scientists will soon publish the new evidence (they have acquired the evidence).

    e. Much of the information about future earthquakes (newspapers publish the information) is actually just speculation.

2. Write an object adjective clause to describe the underlined word in each of the following sentences.

    a. Here are the <u>charts</u>.

    b. I need access to the <u>reports</u>.

    c. The reports highlight the <u>problems</u>.

    d. The government has surveyed the <u>damage</u>.

    e. Pat selected the <u>equipment</u>.

For Discussion and/or Writing

1. Definitions, serious or silly, often use adjective clauses.

   Examples: A telescope is an instrument that is used to study stars.
   A lens is a curved piece of glass that makes things look bigger or smaller.
   A giraffe is an animal that was designed by a committee.

   Working with a partner or small group, write definitions for the following terms:

   a. A fax machine

   b. A microwave

   c. A sphere

   d. A family

   e. A good friend

2. Most people find that there are small things that annoy them in life, and if we keep our eyes and spirits open, we can also usually identify small joys that easily escape our notice. Identify some of your pet peeves and some of the small blessings that come into your life.

   Examples: It's a joy to receive a phone call from a friend whom I haven't seen for months.
   People who talk very loudly on cell phones in public places are annoying.

Preposition Adjective Clauses

For many people, the most difficult adjective clauses are preposition adjective clauses. In these clauses, a relative pronoun takes the place of the object of a preposition. If an adjective clause has a verb that takes a preposition, the preposition cannot be omitted.[3] There are two ways to form these clauses.

Method 1

Two Sentences	One Sentence with an Adjective Clause
Here is the book. I was looking for the book.	Here is the <u>book</u> that I was looking for. ↑ (book)
The man contributes money to our school. I talked to the man.	The <u>man</u> that I talked to contributes money to our school. ↑ (man)

Notice:

1. *Who, whom,* and *that* may be used for people; *which* and *that* may be used for things.
2. The preposition "stays behind" and is right after the verb in the adjective clause.
3. Don't omit the preposition. There is a big difference in meaning, for example, between "the room that I was eating in" and "the room that I was eating" and between "the woman that I was looking for" and "the woman that I was looking at."
4. The relative pronoun may be omitted from this type of preposition adjective clause, because the pronoun isn't a subject.

   Examples: Here is the book I am looking for.
   The man I was talking to contributed money to our school.

---

3. The preposition may be a true preposition or a *particle,* part of a two-word verb (e.g., *up* in the sentence "This is the word that she looked up in her dictionary").

Method 2

Two Sentences	One Sentence with an Adjective Clause
Here is the book. I was looking for the book.	Here is the <u>book</u> for which I was looking. ↑ (book)
The clerk was very helpful. I bought my stereo from the clerk.	The <u>clerk</u> from whom I bought my stereo was helpful. ↑ (clerk)

Notice:
1. The preposition is next to the word that the adjective clause modifies.
2. Only *whom* (for people) and *which* (for things) may be used.
3. This pattern is more common in formal writing than in speech.
4. The relative pronoun may never be omitted from this type of preposition adjective clause.

Practice Exercises

1. Rewrite each of the following sentences, making a preposition adjective clause from the clause in parentheses.

   Example: The story (I alluded to the story) is in this article.
   The story that I alluded to is in this article.

   a. The article (the professor commented on the article) was published last week.

   b. The information (you are looking for the information) can be found on the Web.

   c. The report (this data will be incorporated into the report) is due in March.

2. Write a preposition adjective clause to describe the underlined word in each of the following sentences. Some VERB + PREPOSITION combinations you can use follow.

listen to	talk with	consent to	interact with	register for
transfer to	think about	allude to	look for	be interested in

Example: The <u>program</u> was interesting.
                 The program that I listened to was interesting.

a. Dr. Adams approved of the <u>plan</u>.

b. The <u>class</u> meets on Thursday.

c. The <u>people</u> have lots of innovative ideas.

d. The <u>plan</u> may improve emergency communication significantly.

3. With a partner, ask and answer questions, using phrases from the following list.

am interested in	am excited about	am afraid of	look forward to
am expert at	am impressed by	am frustrated by	am depressed by
insist on	never consent to	like to focus on	react negatively to

Example: What is something <u>that you are interested in</u>?
                 One thing <u>I'm interested in</u> is bird watching.

Other Patterns

Preposition adjective clauses are somewhat complicated to produce. Nearly a thousand years ago, English speakers began avoiding them in certain situations.

Instead of saying:		Speakers say:		Or they say:
the year in which we met	→	the year when we met	→	the year we met
the day on which we came	→	the day when we came	→	the day we came
the time at which we eat	→	the time when we eat	→	the time we eat

Instead of saying:		Speakers say:
the shelf on which I put my books	→	the shelf where I put my books
the drawer in which I put my books	→	the drawer where I put my books
the place at which I put my books	→	the place where I put my books

When you use *where* or *when,* you don't have to remember which preposition to use because you can omit the preposition. This simplification works only when you are using *where* (location) or *when* (time). In other situations, you must keep the preposition.

Practice Exercises

1. Combine each of the following sets of clauses into one sentence, making an adjective clause using *where* or *when* from the clause in parentheses.

   a. Seattle is a city. (People drink a lot of coffee there.)

   b. The town was quite small. (I was born in the town.)

   c. There was a time. (People always knew their neighbors.)

   d. I want to find a time and date. (We can meet at that time and date.)

2. Tell a little about yourself by completing the following sentences using *where* or *when.*

   a. I want to find a place . . .

   b. I remember the time . . .

   c. My hometown is a city . . .

Restrictive versus Nonrestrictive Adjective Clauses

Sometimes you should put commas around adjective clauses.

Examples: Robert Fulton, who invented the steam engine, was an engineer.
My English class, which I enjoy immensely, meets at 11:30 A.M.
My brother Ken, who plays the bassoon, lives in Portland.

Commas are used when the writer believes that the reader knows, even before reading the adjective clause, exactly which person (class, brother, etc.) the writer is talking about. The commas act like small parentheses and indicate that the adjective clause contains "extra" information. Such clauses are called *nonrestrictive adjective clauses*. Observe the following guidelines when you use a nonrestrictive adjective clause.

Don't use *that*.
Don't omit the relative pronoun *(who, whom, which)*.

Sometimes you should not put commas around adjective clauses.

Examples: The person who invented the steam engine was a genius.
The class that I want to take meets at 11:30 A.M. daily.
My brother who plays soccer lives here, but my brother who plays the bassoon lives in Portland.

Commas are not used when the reader needs the information in the adjective clause to identify exactly which person (class, brother, etc.) the writer is talking about. Such clauses are called *restrictive adjective clauses*.[4]

Practice Exercise

Add an adjective clause to each of the following sentences to modify the underlined noun phrase. In each case, decide whether you want to use a restrictive or a nonrestrictive clause.

1. <u>Leonardo da Vinci</u> lived from 1452 to 1519.

2. <u>The Statue of Liberty</u> was a gift from France to the United States.

---

4. Some style guides and computerized grammar checkers say that *which* should never be used in a restrictive relative clause. However, native speakers regularly use *which* in restrictive clauses. Biber et al., in *The Longman Grammar of Spoken and Written English*, report that *which* restrictive clauses are more common than *that* restrictive clauses in 70 percent of academic texts.

3. I never want to meet a <u>criminal</u>.

4. <u>Criminals</u> are very dangerous.

Adjective Clauses with *Whose*

Adjective clauses can also be formed using the possessive pronoun *whose*.

Two Sentences	One Sentence with an Adjective Clause
This is the professor. The professor's class meets in room 106.	This is the <u>professor</u> whose class meets in room 106. ↑ (professor's)
The class is reading a book. The book's author is quite radical.	The class is reading a <u>book</u> whose author is quite radical. ↑ (book's)
Dr. Lee met with students. He had rejected their proposals.	Dr. Lee met with <u>students</u> whose proposals he had rejected. ↑ (students')
The woman is speaking today. We talked about her book.	The <u>woman</u> whose book we talked about is speaking today. ↑ (woman's)

Notice:
1. *Whose* is used with both people and things.
2. A phrase using *whose* can be a subject, object, or object of a preposition.

Practice Exercises

1. Combine each of the following sets of clauses into one sentence, making an adjective clause using *whose* from the clause in parentheses.

   a. Ann is an author. (Her books sell very well in Europe.)

   b. Ted is a journalist. (We respect his work.)

   c. Lee attends a school. (The school's founder was Thomas Jefferson.)

2. Write an adjective clause using *whose* to modify the underlined noun in each of the following sentences.

   a. We talked to the <u>newspaper reporter</u>.

   b. The government subsidizes <u>businesses</u>.

   c. We need a <u>president</u>.

For Discussion and/or Writing

1. We don't always have control over who will or won't be an important part of our lives. Most people, however, try to spend a lot of time around people they like and avoid time with people they find difficult or discouraging. What kind of people do you try to spend time with? Are there kinds of people you try to avoid? What are some specific characteristics of people you want to spend time with? What do you hope to gain by spending time with this kind of person? Try to use some adjective clauses in your discussion.

2. In many communities, there are impressive monuments to people who were famous writers or poets or who were important political leaders. Sometimes there are monuments to people who did unusual things. Think of someone who did something significant but did not receive much recognition (an "unsung hero"). Who was this person? Why do you think there should be a monument to him or her?

Other Uses of *Which* Clauses

Many English speakers use clauses beginning with *which* to comment on ideas and events. In each of the following examples, the *which* clause comments on the preceding clause (not the preceding noun).

> I lost my umbrella this morning, which is very annoying.
> Pam won't cooperate with Mary, which shows that Pam isn't a good team player.

Some speakers use *which* clauses to comment on several sentences at once.

Example: The computer program I'm using isn't compatible with the software that Lee is using. We can't share files. Every time I send Lee a document, it comes out as a mixed up mess, and I lose all my work. Which is why I hate computers.

All good writers know that they must be very careful about using this kind of clause, and most good writers recommend not using them at all. It is very easy to confuse a reader with this kind of clause, because the reader has to guess whether the clause comments on one sentence, two sentences, or a whole paragraph.

Adjective Clauses with *of Which* or *of Whom*

Academic writers often use the phrases *of which* and *of whom,* instead of *whose,* to comment on specific features of something. This style is formal and is rare in conversation.

Two Sentences	Two Ways to Make Adjective Clauses
Governments often invest in new weapons. The cost of new weapons is enormous.	Governments often invest in new weapons, the cost of which is enormous. Governments often invest in new weapons, whose cost is enormous.
Other governments invest in education. The benefits of education are substantial.	Other governments invest in education, the benefits of which are substantial. Other governments often invest in education, whose benefits are substantial.
A scholar is researching the benefits of education for girls. I have forgotten the name of the scholar.	A scholar, the name of whom I have forgotten, is researching the benefits of education for girls. A scholar whose name I have forgotten is researching the benefits of education for girls.

Clauses with *of which* and *of whom* can also be used to comment on a number or amount.

Two Sentences	One Sentence with an Adjective Clause
My teachers don't earn huge salaries. All of my teachers are very capable instructors.	My teachers, all of whom are very capable instructors, don't earn huge salaries.
I have six homework assignments this week. Four of the assignments are interesting.	I have six homework assignments this week, four of which are interesting.

Notice: A clause with *of which* or *of whom* should always be set off from the rest of the sentence by commas.

Practice Exercise

Combine each of the following sets of clauses into one sentence, making an adjective clause using *of which* or *of whom* from the clause in parentheses.

a. Emily Dickinson produced a large body of poetry. (Much of her poetry remained unpublished during her lifetime.)

b. Now her poems are appreciated by thousands of people. (Many of the people memorize them in school.)

c. A complete compilation of Dickinson's poems was published in 1955. (The editor of the compilation was Thomas Johnson.)

For Discussion and/or Writing

1. Think of a historical figure who was, in your opinion, interesting, admirable, or despicable. Tell about that person's character and life.
2. It is said that it is important to make a good first impression. Describe a time when you gave someone the wrong first impression, or describe a time when you got a wrong initial impression of someone else. What happened? How did you correct the wrong impression?

3. What is one problem we are now facing that could be solved by increased commitment to the use of modern technology? Do you think it would be worth the investment (or taxes) it would take to start using that technology?

Chapter 12
Noun Clauses

Introductory Focus

A *noun clause* is a kind of dependent clause. Look at the following proverbs and sentences from popular culture.

> Say what you mean, and mean what you say.
> You get what you pay for.
> What goes around comes around.
> What you don't know can't hurt you.
> Never put off until tomorrow what you can do today.
> Whoever gossips to you will gossip about you.

Have you heard any of these sentences? Do you understand them? Do you agree with some of them? Do you disagree with some of them? What do you notice about the structure of these sentences? How many clauses does each sentence contain? Where are the subjects and verbs in each sentence?

Noun Clauses with Question Words

A noun or noun phrase may fill many roles in a sentence, including subject, object, complement, or object of a preposition. Clauses are sometimes used in these same places. Such clauses are traditionally called noun clauses.[1] Examples of one kind of noun clause—clauses using question words—follow.

---

1. In some texts, these may be called *embedded questions, free relatives, headless relatives, relative adverbs without head nouns,* wh-*clefts, noun complement clauses,* and *noun clauses in apposition,* depending on the type of noun clause.

Noun Phrase	Noun Clause
<u>Lia's report</u> is interesting.	<u>What she said</u> is interesting.
I like <u>classical music</u>.	I like <u>what the orchestra played</u>.
This is <u>our residence</u>.	This is <u>where we live</u>.
I'm interested in <u>storms</u>.	I'm interested in <u>how storms develop</u>.
Les asked <u>a question</u>.	Les asked <u>whether class was canceled</u>.

Notice:
1. Noun clauses that use question words can be used as subjects, objects, complements, or objects of prepositions. They can begin or end sentences.
2. Noun clauses which begin with question words do not use the word order of a question; the subject comes before the verb.
3. When a noun clause with a question word is used as a subject, it takes a singular verb.

Practice Exercises

1. Correct the errors in the following sentences.

   a. I know where is the library.

   b. What Les and Tim are studying are important.

   c. Les is involved in research on how much leisure time do Americans have now.

2. Accuracy practice: Compose sentences using the following words. Add words and change any word forms as necessary.

   a. how / AIDS virus / suppress / immune system / be / not / fully / understood

   b. why / there / upsurge / volcanic activity / be / subject / research

   c. what / psychologist / discover / be / quite / interesting

   d. which / projects / will / succeed / be / difficult / predict

   e. when / investigators / finish / is / unknown

3. Tell something about yourself by completing each of the following sentences with a different noun clause beginning with a question word.

a. I'm interested in . . .

b. I care about . . .

c. I take pride in . . .

d. I wonder . . .

e. I don't understand . . .

If Noun Clauses

The word *if* can be used to begin noun clauses and has about the same meaning as *whether.* There are some limitations on the use of *if* to begin noun clauses.

Whether Noun Clause	*If* Noun Clause
I wonder <u>whether it will rain</u>. Do you know <u>whether or not Sue was at the meeting</u>? <u>Whether or not people can speak freely</u> is an important issue. I'm interested in whether Ted will run for president.	I wonder <u>if it will rain</u>. Do you know <u>if Sue was at the meeting</u>?

Notice:
1. Good writers don't use the word *if* in a noun clause that begins a sentence, because clauses beginning with *if* look like conditional clauses and might confuse the reader.
2. Good writers don't use an *if* clause after a preposition.

That Noun Clauses

A noun clause can begin with the word *that*.

Noun Phrase	Noun Clause
I know <u>the answer</u>.	I know <u>that Geneva is in Switzerland</u>.
	I know <u>Geneva is in Switzerland</u>.
The problem is <u>money</u>.	The problem is <u>that I don't have unlimited funds</u>.
	The problem is <u>I don't have unlimited funds</u>.
<u>Sam's wealth</u> is well known.	<u>That Sam is rich</u> is well known.

Notice:
1. Noun clauses beginning with *that* can be used as subjects, objects, or complements. *That* noun clauses cannot be used after prepositions.
2. The word *that* cannot be omitted from a noun clause at the beginning of a sentence because the listener/reader will become confused about the structure of the sentence.

   NOT ENGLISH   Sam is rich is well known.

3. Although the word *that* can often be omitted in a noun clause that does not begin a sentence, it is usually better, in writing, to keep *that*.

Practice Exercise

In business and academic settings, noun clauses are often used to politely express irritations, worries, or concerns. Use *that* noun clauses to complete the following sentences.

Examples: What concerns me is *that we don't have much time to finish the project.*
What bothered Dr. Von was not *that the report was late* but *that it was inaccurate.*

a. What worries us is . . .

b. What frustrates me is . . .

c. What upset me was . . .

d. What discouraged them was . . .

e. What annoyed her was . . .

That Noun Clauses versus Noun Clauses with Question Words

That noun clauses and clauses beginning with question words are not always interchangeable.

The verb *wonder* is always followed by a noun clause with a question word (probably because we wonder about questions).

Examples: We're wondering what questions will be on the test.
             I wonder why imports are rising.

   NOT ENGLISH   I wonder that imports are rising.

The verb *seem* is followed by a *that* noun clause.

Examples: It seems that the laboratory is closed.
             It seems strange that no one noticed the theft for three days.

   NOT ENGLISH   It seems why the laboratory is closed.

The verb *know* may be followed by either a noun clause with a question word or a *that* noun clause, depending on the meaning intended.

Examples: I know that the phenomenon occurred.
             I know why the phenomenon occurred.

It is important to think about the meaning of the sentence you are writing. If you are unsure about which forms are appropriate after a particular verb, consult the entry for the verb in a good learner's dictionary.

Practice Exercises

1. Complete each of the following sentences with a *that* noun clause or a noun clause with a question word.

   Examples: I need to know *why the report is late.*
   Circumstances dictated *that we postpone the meeting.*

   a. Our professor stressed . . .

   b. What I want to know is . . .

   c. I don't comprehend . . .

   d. There is some dispute as to . . .

   e. There is no denying . . .

   f. Some people never seem to learn . . .

   g. We can assume . . .

2. Using data from the table, complete each of the following sentences with a *that* noun clause or a noun clause with a question word.

Percent of Adult Population Doing Volunteer Work: 1998

[Volunteers are persons who worked in some way to help others for no monetary pay during the previous year. Based on a sample survey of 2,553 persons 18 years old and over conducted during the spring of the following year and subject to sampling variability; see source]

Age, sex, race, and Hispanic origin	Percent of population volunteering	Average hours volunteered per week	Educational attainment and household income	Percent of population volunteering	Average hours volunteered per week	Type of activity	Percent of population involved in activity
Total.	55.5	3.5	Elementary school . . .	29.4	(B)	Arts, culture, humanities. .	8.6
			Some high school. . . .	43.0	3.9	Education	17.3
18-24 years old	48.5	3.0	High school graduate .	43.2	2.8	Environment	9.2
25-34 years old	54.9	3.5	Technical, trade, or			Health.	11.4
35-44 years old	67.3	3.7	business school	53.5	3.5	Human services	15.9
45-54 years old	62.7	3.8	Some college	67.2	4.8		
55-64 years old	50.3	3.3	College graduate	67.7	3.1	Informal	24.4
65-74 years old	46.6	3.6				International, foreign	2.5
75 years old and over.	43.0	3.1	Under $10,000.	42.1	3.4	Political organizations . . .	4.6
			$10,000-$19,999	42.2	2.9	Private, community	
Male	49.4	3.6	$20,000-$29,999	43.7	4.0	foundations	3.4
Female	61.7	3.4	$30,000-$39,999	54.4	3.4		
			$40,000-$49,999	67.5	3.6	Public and societal benefit.	7.9
White.	58.6	3.5	$50,000-$59,999	62.8	4.3	Recreation - adults	8.6
Black.	46.6	4.7	$60,000-$74,999	71.2	2.9	Religion	22.8
			$75,000-$99,999	64.2	3.5	Work-related organizations	10.3
Hispanic [1]	46.4	2.1	$100,000 or more. . . .	70.5	3.5	Youth development	17.5

B Base figure too small to meet statistical standards for reliability.   [1] Hispanic persons may be of any race.

Source: Saxon-Harrold, Susan K.E., Murray Weitzman, and the Gallup Organization, Inc., *Giving and Volunteering in the United States: 1999 Edition.* (Copyright and published by INDEPENDENT SECTOR, Washington, DC, 2000.)

Table reprinted with permission.

a. This information indicates . . .

b. I don't understand . . .

c. . . . appears important.

d. . . . is thought-provoking.

e. I want to know . . .

It Sentences with Noun Clauses

Although using a *that* noun clause as a subject of a sentence is perfectly grammatical, English speakers often avoid this kind of sentence, especially if the noun clause is a long one. One common way of avoiding this kind of sentence is to use *it* as the subject and put the *that* clause later in the sentence, after the verb or a predicate adjective.

Noun Clause as Subject	*It* as Subject
That costs are rising worries me.	It worries me that costs are rising.
That imports are rising is significant.	It is significant that imports are rising.

Notice: Good writers don't use noun clauses with question words in sentences with *it* as the subject.

Practice Exercise

Change the following sentences into sentences with *it* as the subject.

1. That volunteering is an important part of American culture is well documented.

2. That volunteering increases with income is clear.

3. That many low-income individuals also volunteer each week surprises some people.

For Discussion and/or Writing

1. Describe a volunteer project that you have participated in. What did you learn from the project? What aspects of the experience were meaningful to you? Why?
2. In many cultures, volunteer work is not part of ordinary life. If you know one of those cultures, discuss what you know about why volunteering is not important in it.
3. What volunteer work would you like to do in the future?

Noun Clauses as Complements

Noun Clauses as Complements of Nouns

That noun clauses are used after some nouns to complete or define the meaning of the noun.[2]

Examples: The way <u>that Leo solved the problem</u> was quite innovative.
There is no guarantee <u>that our revenue will be adequate for our needs</u>.
Sue has a notion <u>that she will become a famous movie star someday</u>.
Ron borrowed money on the assumption <u>that he could pay it back easily</u>.

Notice:
1. The noun clause in each of the preceding examples completes (defines) the meaning of the noun that it follows.
2. Only some nouns can be completed (defined) by a noun clause.
3. When placed after a noun, a noun clause looks very much like an adjective clause.
4. There are differences between complement noun clauses and adjective clauses. A noun clause uses *that*, never *which*. *That* serves as a connector but is not the subject or object of the noun clause. (These differences in definition are not important to most students, unless they want to become linguists or grammarians.)

   Examples: The report <u>that Omicron Corporation lost money</u> discouraged Sue. (noun clause)
   $$S \quad V \quad O$$

   The report <u>that Tom wrote</u> discouraged Sue. (adjective clause)
   $$O \quad S \quad V$$

---

2. This kind of noun clause is sometimes called an *appositive noun clause.*

Practice Exercise

Complete each of the following sentences with a complement noun clause.

1. I like the way that . . .

2. The belief that . . . is important in many people's lives.

3. Many people agree with my opinion that . . .

The Fact That

The word *fact* is often followed by a complement noun clause, and sentences with the phrase *the fact that* are common.

Examples: The fact that alcohol kills living cells is well known.
Are you aware of the fact that the European Union began using only one currency, the euro, in 2002?
My colleagues at work appreciate me due to the fact that I have a positive attitude.

Some good writers think that the phrase *the fact that* is ugly and recommend avoiding it. Very often, you can omit *the fact* and still have a good sentence. However, *that* clauses cannot be used after a preposition. If you must use a preposition, you will need to keep the phrase *the fact that*.

Examples: That alcohol kills living cells is well known.
Are you aware that the European Union began using only one currency, the euro, in 2002?
My colleagues at work appreciate me because (or due to the fact that) I have a positive attitude.

Noun Clauses as Complements of Adjectives

Noun clauses are also used after some adjectives.

Examples: I am sure <u>that the police conducted a thorough investigation of the robbery</u>.
Everyone is happy <u>that crime rates in the United States are going down</u>.
We are sorry <u>that we are obliged to terminate our agreement with the Sigma Corporation</u>.

Notice: Only some adjectives can be completed with a noun clause. If you are unsure whether a complement noun clause is possible with a particular adjective, consult the entry for the adjective in a good learner's dictionary.

Practice Exercises

1. Complete each of the following sentences with a complement noun clause.

   a. I am glad . . .

   b. I'm sorry . . .

   c. I am proud . . .

   d. Our instructor is pleased . . .

2. Many of the famous speeches and documents of American history contain noun clauses. Analyze the following selections. Underline the noun clauses. (Some of the punctuation has been changed from the original to match modern styles.)

   From the Declaration of Independence, July 4, 1776
   We hold these truths to be self-evident: that all men are created equal; that they are endowed by their creator with certain unalienable rights; that among these are life, liberty, and the pursuit of happiness; that to secure these rights, governments are instituted among men, deriving their just powers from the consent of the governed; that whenever any form of government becomes destructive of these ends, it is the right of the people to alter or to abolish it and to institute new government, laying its foundation on such principles and organizing its powers in such form as to them shall seem most likely to effect their safety and happiness.

   From John Kennedy's inaugural address, January 20, 1961
   We dare not forget that we are the heirs of that first revolution.
   We shall always hope to . . . remember that, in the past, those who foolishly sought power by riding the back of the tiger ended up inside.
   And so, my fellow Americans, ask not what your country can do for you; ask what you can do for your country. My fellow citizens of the world, ask not what America will do for you, but what, together, we can do for the freedom of man.

From Martin Luther King Jr.'s speech *I Have a Dream,* August 28, 1963
    When the architects of our republic wrote the magnificent words of the Constitution and the Declaration of Independence, they were signing a promissory note to which every American was to fall heir. This note was a promise that all men, yes, black men as well as white men, would be guaranteed the unalienable rights of life, liberty and the pursuit of happiness.

For Discussion and/or Writing

1. What are some rights that you think are self-evident?
2. What are some lessons from history that you think we should remember?
3. What beliefs about living a meaningful life are particularly important to you?

The Formal Sequence of Tenses for Reported Speech

Noun clauses are often used to report what someone has said (reported speech). If the reporting verb (e.g., *say*) is in past tense, careful writers use the formal sequence of tenses which is presented in the following chart.

Direct Quote		Reported Speech
simple present tense	→	simple past tense
Sue said, "My schedule is flexible."		Sue said that her schedule was flexible.
present continuous tense	→	past continuous tense
Lee said, "Tom is editing the report."		Lee said Tom was editing the report.
simple past, present perfect, or past perfect tense	→	past perfect tense
Kim said, "Dr. Lee authored a book." Kim said, "Dr. Lee has authored a book." Kim said, "Dr. Lee had authored a book."		Kim said that Dr. Lee had authored a book.
future time	→	"future in the past" form
Sue said, "I am sure we will win."		Sue said she was sure they would win.
Sue said, "The team is going to win."		Sue said the team was going to win.

Direct Quote		Reported Speech
command	→	infinitive
Jim said to Sue, "Revise your essay."		Jim told Sue to revise her essay.
yes/no question	→	*if* clause
Jim asked, "Is this label accurate?"		Jim asked if the label was accurate.
wh-question	→	noun clause
Pat asked, "Where is the label?"		Pat asked where the label was.

Time and place expressions also change in reported speech.

Expression in Direct Quote		Expression in Reported Speech
now, today	→	*then, at that time, that day*, etc.
tomorrow, next week, next month	→	*the next day, the following week, a month later*, etc.
yesterday, last week, a year ago	→	*the previous day, the week before, a year earlier*, etc.
here	→	*there*

If the reporting verb is in present tense (indicating either present or future time), the tense in the noun clause does not change.

Examples: Sue always says, "My schedule is flexible." → Sue says her schedule is flexible.

Pam will complain, "The teachers assign too much homework." → Pam will complain that the teachers assign too much homework.

If the reported speech states a fact or general principle, if the report is made immediately after the original statement, or if the report speaks of an event that is still in the future, many speakers do not change the form of a noun clause verb into past tense.

Examples: Dee said that Tokyo is the capital of Japan.

Pat: "I couldn't hear Leo. What did he say?"

Kim: "He asked what time it is."

Ted said that he will travel to Europe next year.

Practice Exercise

Read the following direct quotation and then complete the four sentences that follow. Use the formal sequence of tenses for reported speech.

Jan said, "I have often used the Internet to research volunteer organizations. For example, last month, I used the Habitat for Humanity Web site to find out where their nearest projects are located. I am also interested in environmental issues, and I search the Internet for information on volunteer opportunities in parks and national forests. I am hoping to find a project I can participate in somewhere near my home."

1. Jan said that . . .

2. She specified that . . .

3. She also reported that . . .

4. Finally, she stated that . . .

Chapter 13
Subjunctive Verb Forms

Introductory Focus

A thousand years ago, English had a verb tense that is now rarely used. Called *subjunctive*, it was used when the speaker wanted to communicate that an event was imagined, wished for, or unreal. While subjunctive forms were once common, Modern English has only a few remnants of this tense. If some of the verb forms in this unit seem a little strange, it is because they are the last examples of a tense that has nearly disappeared.

Look at the following sayings.

> If something sounds too good to be true, it probably is.
> Life is great if you don't weaken.
> If wishes were horses, beggars would ride.
> If fools wore white caps, we would all look like geese.
> If money could talk, it would say good-bye.

Have you heard any of these sayings? What do they mean? Do you agree with them? Look at the verb forms in the sayings. Do any of them seem odd? How?

The following traditional wordplay uses subjunctive verb forms. Do you understand it?

> How much wood would a woodchuck chuck if a woodchuck could chuck wood?
> (A woodchuck is a large, squirrel-like animal. The word *chuck* can mean "throw.")

Ordinary Conditionals ("Real" Conditionals)

Conditional sentences express a *condition*, usually in a clause beginning with *if*, and a *result*. Locate the conditions and results in the following sentences.

I get good grades if I study hard.

If prices increase, sales decrease.

If we get a favorable response to our request, we will need to act quickly.

If the speaker of a conditional sentence wishes to communicate that the condition is a real possibility, the verb tenses in the sentence follow the usual rules for verb tenses in adverb and main clauses. Such sentences are used to make a prediction or to state a principle or fact.

Past Time	Present/Future Time
In the 1700s, if a person caught smallpox, he or she usually died.	If Tim knows the answer, he will tell us. If the price of an item increases, the demand for it falls. If you finish the preliminary draft of the report by 3:00 P.M., we can give it to Les at today's meeting.

Occasionally such sentences are used in a way that is not truly conditional.

Examples: There are some apples in the refrigerator if you get hungry. (The apples are in the refrigerator whether or not the hearer gets hungry. The social meaning of the sentence is that the hearer is welcome to the apples in the refrigerator if he or she gets hungry.)

I can finish this report by 2:00 P.M. if you want me to.

If someone gets hurt, there's a first-aid kit in the kitchen.

Practice Exercises

1. Accuracy practice: Compose sentences using the following words. Do not change the order of the words, but add any words or change any word forms as necessary.

   a. if / two / atom / combine / form / molecule

   b. if / have / difficult / goal / must / work / hard

   c. government / will / respond / if / military threat

2. Complete the following sentences as statements of facts or principles.

   a. If a gas is heated, . . .

   b. If a person perpetrates a crime, . . .

   c. If a trait is hereditary, . . .

   d. If you get upset over trivial incidents, . . .

   e. If a person smokes, . . .

3. Complete the following sentences as predictions about the future.

   a. If I pass this class, . . .

   b. If today's weather report is accurate, . . .

   c. If you cease studying for this class, . . .

   d. If I eliminate sleep from my schedule, . . .

   e. If I achieve my goal of getting a degree, . . .

Hypothetical Conditionals ("Unreal" Conditionals): Present/Future Time

If the speaker of a conditional sentence wishes to communicate that the condition is hypothetical (unreal, imagined), the verbs in both clauses of the sentence use special forms.

Examples: If Tim knew the answer, he would tell us. (Implied: Tim doesn't know the answer.)

If we had a million dollars, we could buy the equipment we want for the lab. (Implied: We don't have a million dollars.)

If I had a million dollars, I might spend it all on chocolate. (Implied: I don't have a million dollars.)

If Lee attended class more regularly, his grades would go up. (Implied: Lee doesn't attend class regularly.)

If I were you, I would take Linguistics 440 next quarter. (Implied: I am not you.)

If it weren't raining, we could play tennis. (Implied: It is raining.)

If they were invited, they would come. (Implied: They haven't been invited.)

Notice:

1. The verb in the *if* clause of a hypothetical conditional in present or future time always looks like it is in simple past tense. Technically, it is subjunctive. However, for convenience, many students call it past tense.
2. The verb in the main clause uses *would, could,* or *might.*

   Would makes a prediction.
   Could says the action is not impossible.
   Might expresses the idea "maybe."

3. In formal academic English, the verb *be* always appears in the form *were* in the *if* clause. In informal conversational English, *was* is often used.

Formal	Informal
If Ken were here, he would help us.	If Ken was here, he would help us.
If I were you, I would proofread that proposal before I turned it in.	If I was you, I'd proofread that proposal before I turned it in.

Practice Exercises

1. The following sentences express hypothetical situations. Fill in the blanks in each sentence with appropriate verb forms from the words in parentheses.

   a. I am extremely tired today. I don't want to do anything. If I

   _____ (feel) a little more energetic, I _____ (start)
   work on my paper for my philosophy class.

   b. The Alpha Corporation does not allow any kind of flextime for its
   workers. A lot of workers are leaving for other companies. If the

   corporation _____ (have) a more enlightened attitude, it

   _____ (not lose) so many qualified workers.

   c. Ann doesn't understand the gravity of the situation. If she

   _____ (tell) how serious the problem is, she _____
   (respond) more appropriately.

   d. The Gamma Corporation has very few security rules and no security

   officers. They _____ (have) fewer thefts if they _____

   (institute) more elaborate security precautions.

2. Accuracy practice: Compose sentences using the following words. Do not
   change the order of the words, but add words or change any word forms
   as necessary.

   a. if / population / be / homogeneous / marketing / be / easier

   b. if / company / face / financial / crisis / bank / might / lend / money

   c. I / not / worry / if / I / be / you

   d. production method / be / popular / if / it / not / consume /
   so much / energy

   e. people / get / help / if / public / have / enlightened attitude /
   toward alcoholism

3. Tell a little about yourself by completing the following conditional sentences.

   a. If I had a lot of money, . . .

   b. If I could travel anywhere in the world, . . .

   c. If I had a free day tomorrow, . . .

4. The words *If I were you, I'd* . . . are often used as a formula for giving advice. Working in pairs or small groups, describe several problems and give advice using this formula.

   Examples: Student A: My neighbor plays loud music late at night.
                 Student B: If I were you, I'd buy earplugs.

                      Student A: I don't think I can get this paper done by tomorrow.
                      Student B: If I were you, I'd ask the professor for an extension.

For Discussion and/or Writing

1. Many people do not try to achieve their dreams because they fear failure. What new thing would you try if you had no fear of failure? Why?
2. If you could do only one of the following, which one would you choose? Why?

   Find a cure for all the major mental illnesses (depression, schizophrenia, bipolar disorder)
   Prevent the destruction of the world's forests
   Find a way for every person on earth to get at least a high school education
   Develop a completely safe way to generate unlimited electrical power

3. If you could give a special gift to one person, what would you give and to whom?

Hypothetical Conditionals ("Unreal" Conditionals): Past Time

Speakers use conditionals to express their hypotheses (imagined results, guesses) about the past.

Examples: If Bob had known the answer yesterday, he would have told us. (Implied: Bob didn't know the answer.)

If I had had two weeks to work on the report, instead of two days, I could have done a better job. (Implied: I didn't have two weeks to work.)

If Nan had attended classes more regularly last quarter, she would have learned a lot more than she did. (Implied: Nan didn't attend classes regularly last quarter.)

If we had been warned of the danger, we would not have entered the building. (Implied: We were not warned.)

Notice:
1. The verb in the *if* clause of a hypothetical conditional in past time uses *had* + past participle.
2. The verb in the main clause uses *would have, could have,* or *might have* + past participle. These are subjunctive verb forms, but they look just like past modal forms.
3. In informal spoken English, these verb forms are often contracted. The word *have* may be pronounced like *of* or *a.* In writing, be sure to use *have.*
4. In informal spoken English, speakers sometimes use *would* in the *if* clause. This is not yet acceptable in formal written English.

Informal Spoken English	Formal Written English
If she'd known the answer, she'd of told you.	If she'd known the answer, she would have told you.
If he'd heard the question, he woulda (he'da) answered.	If he'd heard the question, he would have answered.
If you would have told me you needed help, I would have helped you immediately.	If you had told me you needed help, I would have helped you immediately.

Practice Exercises

1. The following sentences express hypotheses about the past. Complete each sentence with appropriate verb forms from the words in parentheses.

   a. If the designers of these offices _____ (use) less intense colors,

      they _____ (achieve) more aesthetically pleasing results.

   b. Authorities are not convinced that the riot was spontaneous. If it

      _____ (be) spontaneous, there _____ (not be) so
      many signs of communication between leaders on different streets.

   c. If the local government _____ (not impose) severe restrictions
      on development some years ago, most of the farmland around here

      _____ (convert) into housing developments and shopping
      malls.

   d. There _____ (not be) so many complaints from employees if

      the workload _____ (distribute) more equitably.

   e. The courts _____ (rule) in their favor if they _____
      (have) a justified complaint, but they didn't.

2. Accuracy practice: Compose sentences using the following words. Do not change the order of the words, but add words or change any word forms as necessary.

   a. if / professor / draw / better / diagram / yesterday / I /
      understand / problem

   b. if / committee / assemble / necessary information / earlier / they /
      finish / report / last week

   c. reporter / be granted / interview / yesterday / if / submit /
      written request

   d. mayor / not / be reelected / if / she / advocate / increased taxes /
      last year

   e. if / companies / accept / government mediator / conflict /
      be solved / quickly

For Discussion and/or Writing

1. Imagine yourself at age 5 or 10. What would you have done if you had had a horse? a bicycle? a chance to visit Disneyland?
2. What advice would you have given if you had met Napoleon? Cleopatra? Genghis Khan? Simón Bolívar? Elvis Presley?
3. What do you think would have happened in Asia, Africa, or South America if European nations had never claimed colonies there?
4. What do you think would have happened in Europe if Germany and the other Axis powers had won World War II?

Hypothetical Conditionals ("Unreal" Conditionals): Mixed Time

Speakers sometimes combine in one sentence an *if* clause about the past with a result clause about the present. In such a sentence, the speaker is imagining the effect of a change in the past on a situation in the present.

Examples: If I had finished my report yesterday, I would not be so pressed for time today.
   If England had not colonized North America, English would not be an important language in the Western Hemisphere.

Notice:
1. The *if* clause of a hypothetical condition in mixed time uses the verb forms that are found in hypothetical conditionals about the past.
2. The result clause uses the verb forms that are found in hypothetical conditionals about the present.

Practice Exercise

The following sentences express hypothetical conditionals in mixed time. Complete each sentence with appropriate verb forms from the words in parentheses.

a. If Don _____ (not take) his wife for granted, he _____ (still be) a married man.

b. This project _____ (be) completed by now if the Office of

Development _____ (not insist) on reviewing our plans in microscopic detail before we began working.

c. If the developers of this program _____ (take) even rudimentary precautions against fraud, we _____ (not face) the problems we do now.

d. If the Lambda Corporation _____ (not build) such a reservoir of goodwill in the community, their current public relations problems

_____ (be) much more serious.

e. If the federal government _____ (not subsidize) so much

housing in the 1980s, communities _____ (deal) with a much larger homeless population today.

For Discussion and/or Writing

1. What would you look like today if you had grown a foot taller yesterday?
2. How would your life be different if television had never been invented?
3. How would your field of study be different today if the Internet had never been developed?
4. What three inventions do you think have been the most beneficial to humanity? How would life today be different if those three things had never been invented?

Hidden and Implied Conditionals

Most conditional sentences contain an *if* clause and are therefore easy to spot. Other conditional sentences are less obvious. Notice the verb forms in the second sentence of each of the following pairs. They express a hypothetical situation.

Past	Present/Future Time
I had to study last night. Otherwise, I would have gone to the concert with you.	I have an important meeting to attend this afternoon. Otherwise, I would go for a walk in the park.
He was at a baseball game. In another context, his shouting would not have been considered appropriate.	The library is closed. Otherwise, I could work on my history paper.
	Ben is suing me in court. In other circumstances, I would invite him to join us for dinner.

Notice:

1. The word *otherwise* communicates in one word the idea "if the situation were different" or "if the situation had been different." A clause that uses *otherwise* expresses a hypothetical idea.
2. Any phrase that communicates the idea "if the situation were different" causes a speaker to use hypothetical (subjunctive) verb forms.

Practice Exercises

1. The following sentences contain hidden conditionals. Rewrite them as conditional sentences using *if*.

   a. This contract requires us to use all natural fabrics. Otherwise, we would use synthetic fabrics here.

   b. In a more homogeneous group, we could reach an agreement more quickly.

   c. In the event that this rain persists, we will forgo our plans for a picnic.

   d. The city allocates a very small proportion of its budget to park maintenance. Under other circumstances, we would be able to replant the flower beds each year.

   e. With a more philosophical approach to his problems, he could have avoided a lot of stress.

2. Complete the following sentences, using subjunctive verb forms.

   a. I am broke. Otherwise I, . . .

   b. We have only 20 minutes to meet today. With more time, we . . .

    c. The government of that country suppresses the people by force. In other circumstances, . . .

    d. Lee insisted on paying for our meal last night. Otherwise, . . .

Although most native speakers don't know the word *subjunctive,* they recognize that a subjunctive verb expresses the belief of the speaker that an event is hypothetical, unreal, or imaginary. Notice the verb tenses in the following sample paragraph.

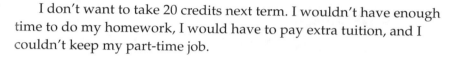

       I don't want to take 20 credits next term. I wouldn't have enough time to do my homework, I would have to pay extra tuition, and I couldn't keep my part-time job.

There is an implied (unspoken) conditional clause after the first sentence: "If I took 20 credits next term, . . ."

When a native listener hears such forms as *wouldn't have, would have to, couldn't,* the native listener knows that the speaker is hypothesizing about the future. Academic writing frequently contains this kind of implied conditional.

Examples: Even a small increase in the average temperature worldwide would have a severe impact on a number of plant and animal species. Some species might become extinct within their current ranges.
          A comprehensive approach to reducing crime would require allocating more resources to social services and economic development.

Practice Exercise

Fill in the blanks in the following sentences, then write two or three more sentences to complete each paragraph. Use implied conditional forms.

a. It's hard to imagine what the modern world _____ be like without private automobiles. Without this form of personal transportation, . . .

b. I hate to think what life _____ be like without doctors, hospitals, and other forms of modern medical care. Under those circumstances, . . .

For Discussion and/or Writing

1. Think of someone who would definitely not be a good choice for a particular job. Imagine what would happen if that person held the job.

    Example: I'm glad my cousin Sue isn't president of the United States. She would insult foreign ambassadors and might burn down the White House with her cigarettes.

2. Explain what would, could, and/or might happen if a natural disaster hit the town where you are now living. (Choose one type of disaster—e.g., earthquake, tornado, hurricane.)

3. If you suddenly received five million dollars, would you stop going to school? Would you change your career plans? If you didn't need money, would you work? Think about your father, uncle, or another man of your father's generation. Would his answers be (or have been) the same as yours? Why or why not?

4. What do you think would be the advantages and disadvantages of establishing a permanent military force under the control of the United Nations?

Rare Forms

The three following patterns are not common but are occasionally used, particularly in academic writing. These patterns just represent differences in style.

The word *should* is occasionally used in ordinary ("real") conditionals in present or future time and is sometimes put before the subject.

Examples: If she should call, I will give her your message.
Should she call, I will give her your message.
(Meaning of both: If she calls, I will give her your message.)

In hypothetical conditionals about the past, the word *had* is occasionally put before the subject.

Example: Had he acted unfairly, he would have compounded the problem.
(Meaning: If he had acted unfairly, he would have compounded the problem.)

Another uncommon form that occurs occasionally in hypothetical conditionals uses *were* + infinitive. The word *were* is sometimes put before the subject.

Examples: If you were to reassess the data, you might come to a different
conclusion.
Were you to reassess the data, you might come to a different
conclusion.
(Meaning of both: If you reassessed the data, you might come to
a different conclusion.)

For Discussion and/or Writing

When a speaker in an academic setting wants to explain that he or she has learned something from an activity and now has a better idea of how to do it, the speaker often introduces this better idea by saying, "Were I to do this over again, I would . . . ," or, "Had I the opportunity to do it over again, I would . . ." Think of a situation where you didn't handle a problem in the best way possible. What would you do differently if you were to do things over again?

Subjunctive Complements

An unusual verb pattern occurs with a small list of verbs which communicate that one person wants another person to do something. The pattern for sentences using these verbs is subject (person 1) + VERB + *that* + subject (person 2) + VERB, as in the following examples.

Present/Future Time	Past Time
I prefer that Zoe come tomorrow rather than today.	They insisted that the project manager attend yesterday's meeting.
The airline suggests that passengers be at the airport two hours before departure.	
The supervisor recommended that Pat not be promoted.	
The lab manager requires that users change passwords every two months.	

Notice:

In a sentence following this pattern, the verb in the second clause (the noun clause, or the *subjunctive complement*) is in its very simplest form. There is no -*s*, -*ed*, -*ing*, or auxiliary verb. The verb *be* is always *be*—never *am, is, are,* et cetera. The word *that* may be omitted, but it is better to keep *that* in written work.

The following verbs can occur in the first clause of such a sentence.

advise	command	move	propose	require
ask	demand	order	recommend	stipulate
beg	insist	prefer	request	suggest

Several related nouns and adjectives follow the same pattern.

Nouns			Adjectives
advice	order	request	essential
command	preference	requirement	imperative
demand	proposal	stipulation	important
insistence	recommendation	suggestion	necessary
			vital

Example sentences follow.

Past Time	Present/Future Time
The proposal that Tom become chairman was accepted.	The requirement that you be on time is reasonable. It is necessary that construction be halted immediately.

The unusual verb pattern in imperative noun clauses is, like the other unusual verb patterns in this chapter, a remnant of the Old English subjunctive tense. It is used only when one person wants another person to do something.

Examples: My boss is very strict. She insists that I be on time every day. (She insists = she demands.)
My boss is not very well educated. She insists that London is the capital of France. (She insists = she says repeatedly and will not change her mind.)

The list of verbs used in this pattern is slowly shrinking over the years. In another century or two, this remnant of the subjunctive tense may disappear completely, but it is still used, perhaps especially in formal academic English.

Practice Exercises

1. Correct the errors in the following sentences.

   a. This contract requires that the stream behind the construction site is restored to its original condition.

   b. The employees' union continues to demand that employees aren't required to work more than six hours of overtime a week.

   c. The directors' insistence that the company transfers its accounts to a new bank was not welcome news to its current bank.

   d. The clients asked that the architect incorporated a home office into the plans for their house.

   e. It is imperative that the dispute between the city council and the firefighters' union is resolved.

2. Complete the subjunctive complement in each of the following sentences.

   a. The requirement that . . . is fair/unfair.

   b. The academic advisors in my department suggest that . . .

   c. A group of students has requested that the school administration . . .

   d. It is vital that a doctor . . .

   e. Mr. Lee's proposal that . . . may help diffuse this crisis.

For Discussion and/or Writing

1. If you could meet with the president of the United States for one hour, what would you advise or suggest that the president do to benefit the nation and the world?
2. What activities and attitudes are essential for a person who wants to lead a good and productive life?
3. When you were a child, what did your parents and teachers demand that you do?

Wish

The verbs *wish* and *hope* both indicate a desire for some situation that is not currently present. The difference is that the verb *hope* communicates that the speaker believes (or wants to believe) that the desired situation is possible and may naturally occur. The verb *wish* communicates that the speaker believes the desired situation is not likely to occur.

When the verb *hope* is followed by a clause, the clause uses ordinary verb forms. When the verb *wish* is followed by a clause, the clause uses subjunctive verb forms. Examples follow.

Present/Future Time	Past Time
I hope your mother will get well soon. I hope the doctor can help her. I wish your mother weren't sick right now. I wish the disease would disappear instantly. I wish I could help you, but I can't. I wish I had more time to work on this report. Everyone wishes Joe would stop talking.	We hoped we could finish the project yesterday. Ana hoped Wes would call her. Yesterday, I wished it would rain. When I was a child, I wished I had red hair.

Notice: In sentences that refer to past time, the verbs after *wish* and after *hope* look the same because subjunctive forms look like past forms.

Practice Exercises

1. For each of the following sentences, compose a new sentence that expresses a wish for the opposite situation.

   Example: It is raining today.
   I wish it weren't raining today.

   a. Learning English takes a lot of time and energy.

   b. Our decisions are dictated by financial constraints.

   c. The director will make a lot of announcements.

   d. This report was released to the press yesterday.

   e. Discretionary funds were eliminated from the budget.

2. Accuracy practice: Compose sentences using the following words. Do not change the order of the words, but add words or change any word forms as necessary.

   a. Lee / hope / that / work / impress / boss

   b. I / wish / that / all / dictator / resign from office

   c. we / wish / that / we / eliminate / disease

   d. I / wish / war / cease

   e. tomorrow / Sue / wish / she / not / spend / money / today

   f. Kim / wish / atomic / weapon / not / be / invent

Wishes about Earlier Times

If a wish refers to a situation that occurred before the time the wish is made, use the verb forms for hypothetical conditionals in past time (*had* + past participle).

Present/Future Time	Past Time
Today, I wish that I had studied harder yesterday. Tomorrow, I will wish that I had studied harder today.	Yesterday, I wished that I had studied harder the day before yesterday.

Practice Exercise

Complete each of the following sentences with the appropriate form of the verb in parentheses.

a. Tom wishes he _____ (buy) a microscope last month.

b. I wish the economy _____ (be) stronger last year.

For Discussion and/or Writing

1. In the folktales of many cultures, there are stories of fairies, genies, leprechauns, and other magic creatures who grant wishes. Imagine that one of these beings is visiting you. Make three wishes.
2. Do you know a folktale about magic wishes? Write or tell it.
3. What do you wish you had done when you were younger?
4. What historical event do you wish had turned out differently?

Other Uses of *Wish*

Occasionally *wish* is used as a synonym for *want* and is followed directly by an infinitive.

Examples: Do you wish to speak with the director?
Students who wish to leave early must get permission from the instructor.
We wish to inform the public that the new Hotel Paradise is open for business.

The word *wish* is used in a number of conventional greetings.

Examples: Best wishes. (This greeting is used at birthdays, weddings, and other celebrations and on greeting cards.)
We wish you a merry Christmas. (This is a line from a popular Christmas song.)
Wish me luck. (This is said when the speaker is about to begin a difficult task.)

Chapter 14
Participial Phrases

Introductory Focus

In English, "light" modifiers usually go before a noun, and "heavy" modifiers go after a noun. One-word adjectives are "light." Phrases and clauses are "heavy." Look at the following sayings.

> A good conscience is a soft pillow.
> A bird in the hand is worth two in the bush.
> A watched pot never boils.
> An open mind is good, but a mind open at both ends is a wind tunnel.
> A person is presumed innocent until proven guilty.

Do you understand these sayings? Do you agree with them? Look at the modifiers in these sayings. Which ones come before a noun? Which ones come after?

English speakers modify nouns with various kinds of phrases. When a phrase begins with a preposition, it is called a *prepositional phrase.*

Examples: We bought a box <u>of chocolates</u>.
               Give the bicycle to the boy <u>with red hair</u>.

When a phrase begins with an adjective, it is called an *adjective phrase.*

Examples: The police station is the building <u>adjacent to the post office</u>.
               The police will arrest the person <u>guilty of this felony</u>.

When a phrase begins with a participle, it is called a *participial phrase.*

Examples: The police recovered items <u>stolen in a robbery</u>.
               The thieves noticed police cars <u>converging on the crime scene</u>.

Adjectival Participial Phrases

Present participles (the *-ing* forms) are often used in phrases that modify nouns. These phrases are called *adjectival participial phrases* or *reduced adjective clauses.*

Sentence	Possible Meanings
The man <u>seeking a wife</u> is Tom.	The man who is seeking a wife is Tom.
Sue is the woman <u>not seeking a husband</u>.	Sue is the woman who is not seeking a husband.
Students <u>majoring in anthropology</u> study many different cultures.	Students who major in anthropology study many different cultures. Students who are majoring in anthropology study many different cultures.
Last year, students <u>majoring in anthropology</u> received scholarships.	Last year, students who were majoring in anthropology received scholarships. Last year, students who majored in anthropology received scholarships.
Vehicles <u>weighing over five tons</u> are prohibited on the bridge.	Vehicles that weigh over five tons are prohibited on the bridge.

Notice:

1. Phrases with present participles (*-ing* forms) have an active meaning.
2. Present participles by themselves are never complete verbs. In the preceding examples, *seeking* and *majoring* are not verbs; they are participials and begin participial phrases.
3. Many participial phrases can be expanded into adjective clauses with approximately the same meaning. If you expand the phrase into a clause, you will need to decide on a tense and add a subject pronoun (*that, which,* or *who*).

Practice Exercise

Underline the participial phrases in the following sentences. What do they mean? (There may be more than one correct way to interpret a phrase.)

a. All rules affecting students are posted in the library.
b. Students must sign a note acknowledging their acceptance of these rules.
c. Students accumulating more than $25.00 in fines will lose library privileges.
d. Any student not adhering to these rules may be dismissed from school.
e. Students damaging school property are liable for the cost of repairs.

Past participles are also often used in phrases that modify nouns.

Sentence	Possible Meanings
A robber underline{captured by the police} is now in jail.	A robber who was captured by the police is now in jail.
There is a reward for the officer underline{credited with catching the thief.}	There is a reward for the officer who is being credited with catching the thief. There is a reward for the officer who was credited with catching the thief.
The police also arrested a man underline{accused of harboring a criminal.}	The police also arrested a man who was accused of harboring a criminal. The police also arrested a man who is accused of harboring a criminal.

Notice:

1. Phrases with past participles have a passive meaning.
2. Because the past participle form and the simple past form of a regular verb are identical, these participials may look like complete verbs. They are not.
3. These phrases, too, can often be expanded into adjective clauses. If you expand the phrase into a clause, you will need to decide on a tense and add *who, which,* or *that*.

Practice Exercise

Underline the participial phrases in the following sentences. What do they mean? (There may be more than one correct way to interpret a phrase.)

a. This book contains poems written by high school students.
b. It is an annual publication devoted to student writing.
c. The stories and poems selected by the editors represent the best of student writing.
d. The editors use a selection process considered very fair to students.
e. The decisions made by a panel of judges are final.

Sometimes participial phrases may look like clauses without subjects. They are not. Be careful. Only participles (not complete verbs) can begin participial phrases, and every complete verb must have a subject.

> NOT ENGLISH   I met a woman has a cat.
> My sister is the girl is sitting in the library.
> A woman was writing a book came to see me.
> There are lots of people have seen this movie.

Restrictive and Nonrestrictive Phrases

Adjectival participial phrases sometimes need commas and sometimes don't. If, in your opinion, the reader knows the reference of the noun (knows which person, thing, etc. you are talking about), use commas around the participial phrase. If, in your opinion, your reader needs the information in the participial phrase in order to identify the reference of the noun, don't use commas.

Examples: The vehicles damaged in the accident can't be repaired.
My brand new motorcycle, damaged in an accident, must be repaired.

Practice Exercises

1. Write six sentences describing some of your favorite foods. Use participial phrases to describe the foods.

   Example: I like a steak covered with onions and accompanied by a baked potato.

   Participials that may work well here include

fried in	coated with	dipped in
soaked in	covered with	marinated in
swimming in	filled with	accompanied by
slathered with	topped with	seasoned with

2. Complete each of the following sentences with a present or past participial form of the verb in parentheses. You will be creating a participial phrase.

   a. Nuclear power generation, _____

   _____ (advocate) by the leaders of several developing nations, presents many safety issues.

   b. Many of the problems _____ (confront) the nuclear power industry seem almost unsolvable.

   c. Regulations _____ (administer) by the Department of Energy cover the training of workers in power plants.

   d. The damage _____ (cause) by the Chernobyl nuclear accident transformed a large part of Ukraine into a wasteland.

   e. Radiation _____ (release) into the air at Chernobyl was detected by monitors in Sweden.

   f. Information about the explosion, _____

   _____ (suppress) in the first weeks after the accident, later came to light.

   g. Areas _____ (select) for processing nuclear waste are usually far away from population centers.

   h. Sites _____ (eliminate) from consideration include any place where earthquakes have occurred.

   i. New techniques for storing nuclear waste, _____

   _____ (develop) in university research labs, may make nuclear power production safer.

3. Combine each of the following pairs of sentences into one sentence in two different ways. First, use an adjective clause. Then, use a participial phrase.

   Example: Homes experience fewer robberies. The homes are equipped with alarm systems.
   Homes that are equipped with alarm systems have fewer robberies.
   Homes equipped with alarm systems have fewer robberies.

a. Our home has an automated alarm system. It was installed by Kappa Security.

b. The system is very high tech. It consists of lights and a siren.

c. The system automatically contacts Kappa Security. It is triggered by sound or motion.

d. Personnel monitor the system 24 hours a day. They work in the head office.

e. A code word activates the system. The code word is entered on a control panel.

Time Relationships in Participial Phrases

Participial phrases don't have tense, but there are ways to indicate time relationships between some participial phrases and a main clause.

Being + Past Participle

Two Sentences	One Sentence with Phrase
The cars are being recalled for repairs. The cars have defective steering mechanisms.	The cars being recalled for repairs have defective steering mechanisms.
The woman was interviewed on TV yesterday. She talked about race cars.	Yesterday, a woman being interviewed on TV talked about race cars.
I talked to the car owner yesterday. The car is being repaired this morning, as I speak.	Yesterday, I talked to the owner of the car being repaired this morning.

Notice:

1. *Being* + past participle emphasizes that a passive action is/was in progress.
2. Usually, the action is/was occurring at the same time as the main clause. Occasionally, in conversation, the action is occurring while the speaker is speaking.

Having + **Past Participle and** *Having Been* + **Past Participle**

Two Sentences	One Sentence with Phrase
Bob put an automatic transmission in his car. Now Bob wants to test-drive the car.	Bob, having put an automatic transmission in his car, wants to test-drive the car.
Dee was taught to drive a race car. Now Dee likes manual transmissions.	Dee, having been taught to drive a race car, now likes manual transmissions.
Ron didn't want to sell his car for $1,500. Ron had been offered $2,000 previously.	Ron, having been offered $2,000 for his car previously, didn't want to sell it for $1,500.
Pat thought $1,500 was too much to pay. Earlier, Pat had appraised the car at $1,000.	Pat, having appraised the car at $1,000, thought $1,500 was too much to pay.

Notice:

1. *Having* makes clear that the action of the participial phrase took place before the time of the main clause of the sentence.[1]
2. *Having* + past participle has an active meaning.
3. *Having been* + past participle has a passive meaning.
4. *Having* sometimes makes a major difference in the meaning of a sentence. Compare the following sentences.

   Joe, sleeping, shouted, "Good morning."
   Joe, having slept, shouted, "Good morning."
   Ana, undergoing surgery, wanted to leave the hospital.
   Ana, having undergone surgery, wanted to leave the hospital.

---

1. This is parallel to the way *have* or *has* + past participle shows that the action took place before the basic time of the speaker's story.

Practice Exercise

Using participial phrases is one way to avoid a series of simple sentences. Combine each of the following pairs of sentences into one sentence by making the first sentence in each pair into a participial phrase.

Example: Pam labored long and hard on her essay. She gave it to her instructor.
Pam, having labored long and hard on her essay, gave it to her instructor.

a. Pam was exposed to liberal political thinking when she was a child. She joined a radical political party when she began her university studies.

b. Pam dedicated the majority of her time to political activities. She emerged as a leader of her party.

c. Pam attained a leadership position. She then decided she didn't agree with her party's ideas.

d. Pam repudiated her liberal political ideology. She joined a conservative political party.

e. Pam was welcomed into the conservative party. She channeled her energy into organizing fund-raising dinners.

For Discussion and/or Writing

1. Are you usually reluctant to ask others for help? How do you react to offers of help? Is it appropriate for someone finding herself/himself in trouble to ask a friend for rescue?
2. What do you think are the most important things a student preparing for college should do?
3. What do you think are some of the most important criteria a student evaluating prospective colleges should consider?
4. In most fields of study and research, people must think about some serious ethical questions. What is one of the ethical issues faced in your field of study? Why is this issue important?

Adverbial Participial Phrases

Participial phrases are sometimes used for purposes other than modifying a noun. In these situations, they are called *adverbial participial phrases* or *reduced adverb clauses*.

Sentence	Possible Meanings
<u>Feeling tired</u>, we stopped to rest.	Because we felt tired, we stopped to rest. While we were feeling tired, we stopped to rest.
I fell asleep <u>sitting in the library</u>.	I fell asleep while I was sitting in the library.
Nan, <u>having finished class</u>, went to the library.	Nan, after she finished class, went to the library. Nan, because she had finished class, went to the library.
<u>Needing money</u>, he will talk to the bank about a loan.	Because he needs money, he will talk to the bank about a loan.
<u>Licensed by the state</u>, teachers must meet state requirements.	Because they are licensed by the state, teachers must meet state requirements.
<u>Exported by Russia</u>, caviar is delicious.	Caviar is exported by Russia. Caviar is delicious.
The store is open daily from 9:00 to 5:00, <u>excluding holidays</u>.[2]	The store is open daily from 9:00 to 5:00. This statement doesn't apply to holidays.

Notice:
1. An adverbial participial phrase may come at the beginning, middle, or end of a sentence.
2. When it comes at the beginning or middle of a sentence, it needs to be set off from the rest of the sentence by commas.
3. When it comes at the beginning of a sentence, it should describe the subject of the sentence.[3]

---

2. Participials like *excluding* are sometimes classified as prepositions.

3. Native speakers often break this rule, but careful writers follow it. A participial phrase at the beginning of a sentence can sound like a joke if it incorrectly describes the subject of the sentence, as in the following examples: "Running down the street, an accident happened"; "While shaving this morning, the mirror broke." Be careful about accidental jokes with participial phrases in other places also, as in "I saw a horse, looking out the window of my house."

4. Adverbial participial phrases must be interpreted in context; the reader has to think about the situation and decide on the meaning. They are often interpreted as cause, and they are sometimes interpreted as indicating time after, while, or when.

5. One particularly useful adverbial phrase is *according to*. Academic writers regularly use this phrase to give the source of their information.

Example: According to Lawrence Summers, education for girls provides many benefits to a community.

Participial phrases may begin with an adverb.

Phrase with Adverb	Phrase without Adverb (Do not delete the adverb—see Notice 2, which follows this box.)
After finishing work, Sue went to a concert.	Finishing work, Sue went to a concert.
While listening to the concert, she fell asleep.	Listening to the concert, she fell asleep.
When falling asleep, I often start to nod.	Falling asleep, I often start to nod.
Before leaving for the concert, we made sure we had our tickets.	(Do not delete the adverb—see Notice 2, which follows this box.)
Ted, since attending the concert, has decided to become a musician.	(Do not delete the adverb—see Notice 2, which follows this box.)
Ann didn't read her program until seated in the auditorium.	(Do not delete the adverb—see Notice 2, which follows this box.)

Notice:

1. If you want to be sure the reader chooses the correct interpretation, you can begin the phrase with *after, while,* or *when*. Participial phrases never begin with *because*.[4]

2. Participial phrases may begin with *before, until,* or *since*. If you mean *before, until,* or *since*, use the adverb. If you don't use it, readers will guess you mean *because, after, when,* or *while*.

---

4. Linguists say that in an English speaker's mental dictionary, the word *because* is marked *because* + subject + VERB. *Because* always begins a clause.

Practice Exercise

Rewrite the following sentences, using a participial phrase instead of an adverb clause.

Example: Because she needed to know what people want to buy, Ann surveyed her customers.
Needing to know what people want to buy, Ann surveyed her customers.

a. Because she enjoys challenges, Ann frequently undertakes new projects.

b. While she was attending college, Ann ran a small business.

c. When she is considering a new business venture, Ann always evaluates its potential for profit.

d. Before she purchased her flower shop, she estimated its potential sales volume.

e. Since she purchased the shop, she has constantly tried to improve it.

Other Participial Phrase Forms

Speakers also use *being* + past participle, *being* + ADJECTIVE, or *being* + NOUN to mean "because (someone/something) is this way."

Examples: Being tired, we decided to rest.
Jon, being interested in railroads, loved visiting the railway museum.
Not being rich, we can't afford a mansion and a yacht.
Pam, being a citizen of Canada, doesn't need a visa to visit the U.S.

Participial phrases sometimes are very short; they can be just one word long.

Examples: A penny saved is a penny earned.
United we stand; divided we fall.

For Discussion and/or Writing

1. It is often said that persistence pays off, meaning that if we are persistent in working toward our goals, we will reap benefits. When have you needed persistence? How has persistence benefited you?

2. People living and working in a new culture often discover that they go through a time of feeling very tired, discouraged, or even depressed. These feelings, often called *culture shock,* can be very hard to cope with. What advice do you have for people experiencing culture shock while adjusting to a new environment?

3. Many families enjoy special recipes handed down from great-grandparents to grandparents to parents. Other families own heirlooms passed from generation to generation. What traditions, objects, recipes, or stories are especially important to your family? Are there items that you would like to pass on to future generations?

4. Usually, constrained by a lack of time and money, we are unable to pursue all of our dreams and goals at once. What goals are of high priority to you right now? Why?

Chapter 15
Readings

Dust
by Sydney King Russell

Agatha Morley
All her life
Grumbled at dust
Like a good wife.

Dust on a table,
Dust on a chair,
Dust on a mantel
She couldn't bear.

She forgave faults
In man and child
But a dusty shelf
Would set her wild.

She bore with sin
Without protest,
But dust thoughts preyed
Upon her rest.

Agatha Morley
Is sleeping sound
Six feet under
The mouldy ground.

Six feet under
The earth she lies
With dust at her feet
And dust in her eyes.

From *Selected Poems (1919–1948)* by Sydney King Russell (Portland: Falmouth Publishing House, 1949).

For Discussion and/or Writing

Analysis Questions

1. This poem contains excellent examples of *irony*, an unexpected twist in meaning or experience. What examples of irony do you notice?
2. Notice the verb tenses. In the first stanza, there is the simple past tense verb *grumbled* and the phrase *all her life*. What does this combination signal about Agatha Morley? Where does the poet shift tenses? Why?

Response Questions

1. Think of another example from history or literature of irony in a person's life. What happened?
2. When someone places excessive emphasis on not-too-important or just plain trivial parts of life, we say that person "majors in the minors." Do you know anyone who majors in the minors? What does that person do? Have you ever been tempted to major in the minors? How? Why?
3. Someday, we will each die and our bodies will turn to dust. Do you think that will be the end of us, or do you think there might be an afterlife? What do you hope will happen to you after you die?

Dust
by Sara Teasdale

When I went to look at what had long been hidden,
   A jewel laid long ago in a secret place,
I trembled, for I thought to see its dark deep fire—
   But only a pinch of dust blew up in my face.

I almost gave my life long ago for a thing
   That has gone to dust now, stinging my eyes—
It is strange how often a heart must be broken
   Before the years can make it wise.

From *Flame and Shadow* by Sara Teasdale (New York: Macmillan, 1920).

Note: The phrase *for I thought to see* is a rare way of saying, "because I thought I would see."

For Discussion and/or Writing

Analysis Questions

1. This poem and the one by Sydney King Russell have identical titles but are very different in tone. How would you describe the differences in tone?
2. This poem says that something that was at one time very important and very painful "has gone to dust now." What do you think the image of "going to dust" means?
3. Study the verb tenses in this short poem. What is the relationship between *went* and *had been hidden* in the first line? Where does the poem change from past tense to present tense? What signals the time change?

Response Questions

1. Are there ways that the years have made you wise about old hurts or problems? Does emotional pain diminish over time, or does it remain strong for many years?
2. Do you know anyone special whom the years have made wise? How did this person gain wisdom? How does this person share wisdom with others?

"Let It Be Forgotten"
by Sara Teasdale

Let it be forgotten, as a flower is forgotten,
    Forgotten as a fire that once was singing gold,
Let it be forgotten for ever and ever,
    Time is a kind friend, he will make us old.

If anyone asks, say it was forgotten
    Long and long ago,
As a flower, as a fire, as a hushed footfall
    In a long forgotten snow.

From *Flame and Shadow* by Sara Teasdale (New York: Macmillan, 1920).

For Discussion and/or Writing

Analysis Questions

1. In your opinion, why did the poet choose the images of a flower, a fire, a footfall, and a snow? What do they have in common?
2. How can time be a kind friend? *An old friend* is a common phrase (collocation) in English. Do you think it is relevant to line 4?

3. In most kinds of writing, the writer's task is to be very precise and clear. If a sentence is ambiguous (has more than one meaning), this is usually a problem. In poetry, however, ambiguity is often good. If a phrase has two meanings, the poet may want us to pay attention to both meanings. Look at the phrase *a fire that once was singing gold* in line 2. Is *singing* part of a present progressive verb phrase *(was singing)*, a participial adjective describing *gold,* or both?

4. Look at the past participles in the poem. Where are they part of passive verb phrases? Where are they participial adjectives?

Response Questions

1. Poets sometimes help us express our own feelings. In what kind of situations might someone quote this poem to a friend?

2. From some people, we often hear the advice "Forgive and forget." Other people say that we can forgive but that it is impossible to forget. What do you think? Are there things that can be forgiven and forgotten? Are there things that can be forgiven but not forgotten? Are there things that can be neither forgiven nor forgotten? Is your perspective different when you need to forgive than when you need to be forgiven?

Reading Prose

The following article and illustrations are taken, with minor adaptations, from the IRIS Consortium Web site and are used with permission. IRIS is a university research consortium dedicated to monitoring the earth and exploring its interior through the collection and distribution of geophysical data. For more excellent materials, see their Web site at <www.iris.edu>. You may want to follow the links to *Education and Outreach* and *Resources.*

Earthquakes
Why Do Earthquakes Happen?

You probably associate earthquakes with destruction caused by falling buildings or by the creation of tidal waves. While earthquakes may be associated with destruction in the time frame of human activity, in the evolution of the Earth they signal the geological forces that build our mountains and create our oceans. In many ways, earthquakes are one of nature's reminders that we are living on the thin outer crust of a planet whose interior is still cooling. Earthquakes happen when parts of Earth's crust move. Big earthquakes occur with movement of about a meter or two. Small earthquakes happen with movements of millimeters.

Earth's outer surface is broken into what geologists call plates. Earthquakes occur when plates move under, over, or slide past each other. On the map below, each dot marks the location of a magnitude 4 or larger earthquake. The earthquakes were recorded over a five year time period. As you can see, most earthquakes occur along the edges of the large plates that make up the Earth's crust. The arrows on the map indicate how fast the plates are moving in millimeters per year—about as fast as your fingernails grow.

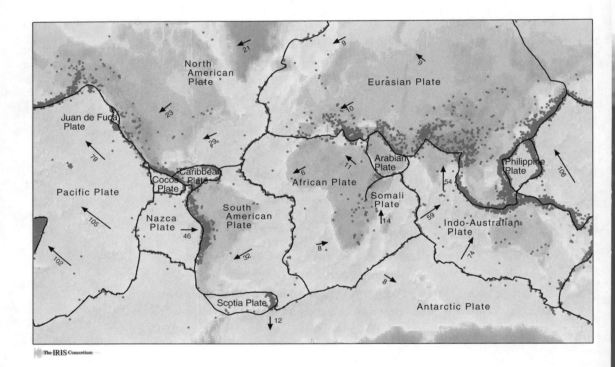

The IRIS Consortium

How Often Do Earthquakes Occur?

Earthquakes are always happening somewhere. Large earthquakes occur about once a year. Smaller earthquakes, such as magnitude 2 earthquakes, occur several hundred times a day. To create a mountain system might take several million medium-size earthquakes over tens of millions of years.

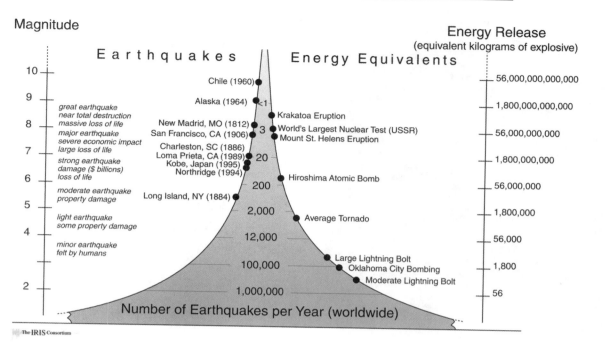

Magnitude

Energy Release
(equivalent kilograms of explosive)

Earthquakes   Energy Equivalents

10	56,000,000,000,000
9	1,800,000,000,000
8	56,000,000,000
7	1,800,000,000
6	56,000,000
5	1,800,000
4	56,000
	1,800
2	56

Chile (1960)
Alaska (1964) <1
great earthquake
near total destruction
massive loss of life
major earthquake
severe economic impact
large loss of life
strong earthquake
damage ($ billions)
loss of life
moderate earthquake
property damage
light earthquake
some property damage
minor earthquake
felt by humans

New Madrid, MO (1812)
San Francisco, CA (1906) 3
Charleston, SC (1886)
Loma Prieta, CA (1989) 20
Kobe, Japan (1995)
Northridge (1994)
200
Long Island, NY (1884)
2,000
12,000
100,000
1,000,000

Krakatoa Eruption
World's Largest Nuclear Test (USSR)
Mount St. Helens Eruption
Hiroshima Atomic Bomb
Average Tornado
Large Lightning Bolt
Oklahoma City Bombing
Moderate Lightning Bolt

Number of Earthquakes per Year (worldwide)

The IRIS Consortium

We describe the size of an earthquake using the Richter Magnitude Scale, shown on the left hand side of the figure above. The larger the number, the bigger the earthquake. The scale on the right hand side of the figure represents the amount of high explosive required to produce the energy released by the earthquake.

The 1994 earthquake in Northridge, California, for example, was about magnitude 6.7. Earthquakes this size occur about 20 times each year worldwide. Although the Northridge earthquake is considered moderate in size, it caused over $20 billion in damage and killed 51 people. The earthquake released energy equivalent to almost 2 billion kilograms of explosive, about 100 times the amount of energy that was released by the atomic bomb that destroyed the city of Hiroshima during World War II, and it raised the Santa Susana Mountains north of Los Angeles by 70 centimeters.

How Can We Use Seismology to Explore the Earth?

Earthquakes create seismic waves that travel through the Earth. By analyzing these seismic waves, seismologists can explore the Earth's deep interior. The Northridge earthquake created seismic waves that ricocheted throughout the Earth's interior and were recorded at geophysical observatories around the world. The paths of some of those seismic waves and the ground motion that they caused are shown below.

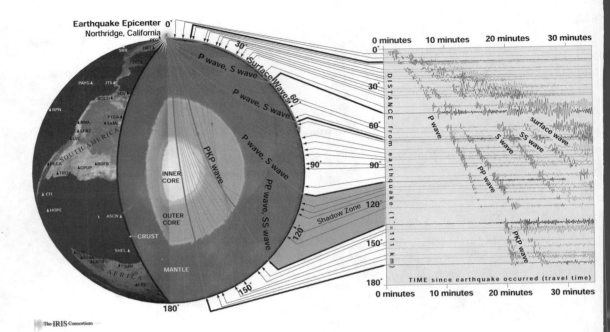

On the right, the horizontal traces of ground motion (seismo-grams recorded at various locations around the world) show the arrival of the different seismic waves. Although the seismic waves are generated together, they travel at different speeds. Shear waves (S waves), for example, travel through the Earth at approximately one-half the speed of compressional waves (P waves). Stations close to the earthquake record strong P, S, and Surface waves in quick succession just after an earthquake occurs. Stations farther away record the arrival of these waves after a few minutes, and the times between the arrivals are greater.

At about 100 degrees distance from the earthquake, the travel paths of the P and S waves start to touch the edge of the Earth's outer core. Beyond this distance, the first arriving wave—the P wave—decreases in size and then disappears. P waves that travel through the outer core are called the PKP waves. They start to appear beyond 140 degrees. The distance between 100 and 140 degrees is often referred to as the "shadow zone."

We do not see shear (S) waves passing through the outer core. Because liquids can not be sheared, we infer that the outer core is molten. We do, however, see waves that travel through the outer core as P waves and then transform into S waves as they go through the inner core. Because the inner core does transmit shear energy, we assume it is solid.

Adapted from three of the "One-Pager" classroom handouts that appear on the resources page of the Education and Outreach Department of IRIS on the IRIS Web site.

For Discussion and/or Writing

Comprehension Questions

1. The earth's crust comprises a number of very large geological plates. What is the relationship between these plates that make up the earth's crust and earthquakes?
2. In the text following the second figure in the article, there is the statement "The larger the number, the bigger the earthquake." What does this mean? (If you have trouble understanding this sentence, see page 98 in chapter 7.)
3. Why does the length of the interval between the arrival of S waves and the arrival of P waves vary by location?
4. S waves can pass through solids but not through liquids. How does this fact help scientists reach conclusions about the internal structure of the earth?

Response Questions

1. (an academic response) The idea that there are large "plates" in the earth's crust (called *plate tectonic theory*) is recent and has had a dramatic impact on the field of geology. In fact, this theory has revolutionized the field. Think about your own area of interest. Choose one idea that has been important in your field. Explain the idea and the impact that it has had.
2. (a personal response) Earthquakes come without warning. They may simply surprise us, or they may cause severe disruption in our lives. Choose one event that came into your life "like an earthquake." What happened? How did this event change your life, in small ways or large?
3. (an imaginative response) There is a famous myth about an island called Atlantis. According to this story, there was once a large island in the Atlantic Ocean that fell to the bottom of the sea in an earthquake, destroying the civilization that existed on the island. Create your own story about a lost civilization. Who were the people? How did they live? How did their civilization end?

The following article is by Dr. Lawrence Summers, who was chief economist at the World Bank at the time he wrote the article. Currently, Dr. Summers is president of Harvard University.

The Most Influential Investment

Educating girls quite possibly yields a higher rate of return than any other investment available in the developing world. Women's education may be unusual territory for economists, but enhancing women's contribution to development is actually as much an economic as a social issue. And economics, with its emphasis on incentives, provides guideposts that point to an explanation for why so many young girls are deprived of an education.

Parents in low-income countries fail to invest in their daughters because they do not expect them to make an economic contribution to the family: girls grow up only to marry into somebody else's family and bear children. Girls are thus less valuable than boys and are kept at home to do chores while their brothers are sent to school—the prophecy becomes self-fulfilling, trapping women in a vicious cycle of neglect.

An educated mother, on the other hand, has greater earning abilities outside the home and faces an entirely different set of choices. She is likely to have fewer, healthier children and can insist on the development of all her children, ensuring that her daughters are given a fair chance. The education of her daughters then makes it much more likely that the next generation of girls, as well as of boys, will be educated and healthy. The vicious cycle is thus transformed into a virtuous circle.

Few will dispute that educating women has great social benefits. But it has enormous economic advantages as well. Most obviously, there is the direct effect of education on the wages of female workers. Wages rise by 10 to 20 percent for each additional year of schooling. Returns of this magnitude are impressive by the standard of other available investments, but they are just the beginning. Educating women also has an impressive impact on health practices, including family planning.

Let us look at some numbers in one country as an illustration of the savings from improved hygiene and birth control. In Pakistan, educating an extra 1,000 girls for an additional year would have cost approximately $40,000 in 1990. Each year of schooling is estimated to reduce mortality of children younger than five years by up to

10 percent. Since an average woman in Pakistan has 6.6 children, it follows that providing 1,000 women with an extra year of schooling would prevent roughly 60 infant deaths. Saving 60 lives with health care interventions would cost an estimated $48,000.

Educated women also choose to have fewer children. Econometric studies find that an extra year of schooling reduces female fertility by approximately 10 percent. Thus, a $40,000 investment in educating 1,000 women in Pakistan would avert 660 births. A typical family-planning evaluation concludes that costs run approximately $65 for each birth averted, or $43,000 for 660 births.

Even beyond those savings, one can calculate that an additional year of schooling for 1,000 women will prevent the deaths of four women during childbirth. Achieving similar gains through medical interventions would cost close to $10,000.

These estimates are of course crude. On one hand, I have failed to discount benefits to reflect the fact that female education operates with a lag. On the other, I have neglected the add-on gains as healthier, better educated mothers have not only healthier, better educated children, but healthier, better educated grandchildren. (When the average mother in Pakistan has nearly 40 grandchildren, that is no small thing.)

Even with these caveats, the social improvements brought about by educating women are more than sufficient to cover its costs. Given that education also yields higher wages, it seems reasonable to conclude that the return on getting more girls into school is in excess of 20 percent, and probably much greater. In fact, it may well be the single most influential investment that can be made in the developing world.

So what can we do to promote investment in the education of girls? Scholarship funds should be established and more free books and other supplies given to girls. Providing schooling that responds to cultural and practical concerns is also essential: female enrollment depends heavily on schools' being nearby, on the provision of appropriate sanitation facilities and on the hiring of female teachers. Flexible hours and care for younger siblings can also be helpful.

Raising the primary school enrollment of girls to equal that of boys in the world's low-income countries would involve educating an extra 25 million girls every year at a total cost of approximately $938 million. Equalizing secondary school enrollment would mean educating an additional 21 million girls at a total cost of $1.4 billion. Eliminating educational discrimination in the low-income countries would thus cost a total of $2.4 billion. This sum represents less than one quarter of 1 percent of the gross domestic product of the low-income countries, less than 1 percent of their investment in new capital goods, and less than 10 percent of their defense spending.

When compared with investments outside the social sector, education looks even more attractive. Take power generation as an example. Projections suggest that developing countries will spend approximately $1 trillion on power plants over the next 10 years. Because of poor maintenance and pricing problems, many of these nations use less than 50 percent of the capability of existing power plants. In a sample of 57 developing countries, the overall return on power-plant physical assets averaged less than 4 percent over the past three years and less than 6 percent over the past decade—returns that cannot even compare with those of 20 percent or more from providing education for females.

No doubt developing countries will improve their efficiency in generating power. And I have probably understated somewhat the difficulty of raising enrollment rates by neglecting capital costs and not taking explicit account of the special costs incurred in targeting girls. Nevertheless, it is hard to believe that building 19 out of every 20 planned power plants and using the savings to finance equal educational opportunity for girls would not be desirable.

There are those who say educating girls is a strategy that pays off only in the long run. This argument reminds me of a story, which John F. Kennedy used to tell, of a man asking his gardener how long it would take for a certain seed to grow into a tree. The gardener said it would take 100 years, to which the man replied, "Then plant the seed this morning. There is no time to lose."

From *Scientific American*, August 1992. Reprinted by permission of Dr. Lawrence Summers.

For Discussion and/or Writing

Comprehension Questions
1. According to the article, what is one reason that parents often send their sons rather than their daughters to school?
2. Each year of schooling corresponds to what increase in wages?
3. How does the author compute the number of infant deaths prevented by providing 1,000 women with an extra year of schooling?
4. What are some things that will help get more girls into school?
5. What is the point of the story about the gardener?

Response Questions

1. (an analytical response) It is usually easier to measure quantity (how much there is of something) than to measure quality (how good something is). In this article, the author attempts to quantify the qualitative benefits of educating girls in developing countries. How do you evaluate his argument? Does it seem convincing to you? Why or why not?

2. (a personal response) In the second paragraph of the article, the author states that some parents see girls as less valuable than boys because, as an adult, a girl will contribute economically to her husband's family, not her birth family. Some people are offended by this logic. They believe that evaluating a person by that person's earning power ignores the intrinsic value of a human being—people are valuable because they are people. What has been your experience? Have you personally seen examples of discrimination or unequal opportunity for persons in various groups? How have you reacted? What do you think should be done?

3. (a research response) Using library or Internet resources, find an answer to one of the following sets of questions.

   a. Since the time this article was written, a number of countries have improved educational opportunities for girls. Where are some of the successful programs? Why have they been successful? Has increased education improved people's lives? (Using the search term "girls education" in a library database or an Internet search engine may help you find some good starting points for your research.)

   b. In this article, the author predicted that governments of developing countries would improve their efficiency in generating power. Has the prediction come true? What are the most promising current ideas for improving electrical production? (Using the search term "electricity AND development" in a library database or an Internet search engine may help you find some good starting points for your research.)

Appendix: Words from the
Academic and University Word Lists

Chapter 1 includes forms of the following words from the Academic and University word lists.

abandon
accommodate
accurate
adjective
aid
alcohol
appreciate
approximate
area
assemble
assignment
available
bond
calendar
capacity
category
chemical
   (chemistry)
civil
clause
clinic
collapse
column
complement
compound
comprise
conduct
conjunction
contradict

convince
coordinate
couple
create
culture
data
define
   (definition)
definite
deliberate
   (deliberately)
demonstrate
   (demon-
   strative)
denote
deviate
distort
domestic
economy
   (economics)
efficient
electron
   (electronic)
eloquent
emotional
emphasis
   (emphatic)
encounter
enormous

episode
equipment
evaluate
exhaust
exhibit
expert
federal
fee
finance
   (financial)
flexible
fluent
fuel
fund
grade
hypothesis
import
impose
inspect
instruct
   (instructor)
intelligent
interview
inverse
   (inversion,
   invert)
issue
laboratory (lab)
leisure

linguistic
   (linguist)
link
locate (location)
medical
minimal
minimize
minimum
ministry
minor
modify
monarch
negative
partner
physical
preliminary
preposition
project
publish
   (publisher)
purchase
reinforce
   (reinforcement)
relax
research
restrict
   (restrictions)
revolve
rural

schedule	style	theory	urban
section	subdivide	tone	usage
sociology	(subdivision)	topic	vocabulary
specify (specific)	symbol	traffic	
stress	technical	transit	
structure	temporary	(transitive)	

Chapter 2 includes forms of the following words from the Academic and University word lists.

accomplish	drama	occur	reject
affect	enormous	overall	schedule
atmosphere	erode	partner	specify (specific)
author	finance	philosophy	switch
channel	focus	plus	tense
chart	impact	precede	theme
column	imply	predict	traditional
comedy	indicate	(prediction)	volunteer
community	initial	primary	
context	interview	principle	
converse	linguistic	professional	
(conversation)	(linguist)	project	
corporate	normal	prosper	

Chapter 3 includes forms of the following words from the Academic and University word lists.

abstract	cater	culture	guarantee
academic	chart	data	guideline
accomplish	clause	define	ignore
acid	client (clientele)	drastic	image
adjust	condense	element	immigrate
adult	confer	(elementary)	(immigrant)
appeal	(conference)	emerge	imply
appropriate	consequent	emphasis	intense
assist	(consequences)	enforce	laboratory (lab)
assure	consult	enhance	levy
astronomy	consume	error	logic (logical)
available	context	estimate	major
biology	contract	focus	negative
bomb	converse	funding	obtain
cancel	(conversation)	furthermore	obvious
capable	create	geography	occur

option
overlap
parenthesis
predict
  (predictability)
preliminary
prohibit
project

psychology
  (psychological)
register
require
research
reside (resident)
role
schedule

sibling
specify (specific)
statistic
  (statistical)
status
stress
submit

survive
  (survival)
symbol
tolerate
trend
visible

Chapter 4 includes forms of the following words from the Academic and University word lists.

academic
access
  (accessible)
accommodate
accomplish
adjective
adult
align
appropriate
chart
civic
coherence
compile
confirm
couple
create
data
derive
design
dispense

display
distribute
document
drain
efficient
estimate
expert
extract
focus
fulfill (fulfilling)
gender
goals
graph
guarantee
hostile
  (hostilities)
ignore
incline
inferior
inflate

institute
interact
invade
invest
  (investment)
investigate
label
layer
link
locate
material
maximize
migrate
negative
oblige
occupy
occur
oxygen
participate
passive

percent
persist
phase
plot
preposition
principle
professional
project
promote
regulate
  (regulations)
require
section
sophisticated
specify (specific)
style
technology
transfer

Chapter 5 includes forms of the following words from the Academic and University word lists.

abstraction
accurate
acquire
adjective
administration
advocate
analogous

analysis
appropriate
author
axis
bond
capable
carbon

catalog
category
chemical
circumstances
cite
communication
community

complicate
comply
comprise
conclusion
consult
contaminate
contemporary

context
converse
   (conversation)
create (creativity)
credible
critic (criticism)
crucial
culture
decade
define
   (definition)
diagram
dispose
distinct
   (distinction)
domain
drug
economy
   (economic)
efficient
element
energy
environment
equipment
error
establish
ethnic
explicit
expose
factor
feature

file
focus
formulate
fundamental
geography
   (geographic)
goal
guideline
hereditary
impact
import
indicate
individual
inhibit
instance
institute
   (institution)
intellect
   (intellectual)
intelligence
intense
interpret
interview
journal
label
laboratory
linguist
locomotion
   (locomotive)
luxury
magnetic

maintain
material
media
minimum
negative
neutral
nutrient
   (nutritious)
paragraph
participate
partner
planet
plot
policy
pollution
precede
preposition
prime
principle
professional
project
pursue
random
region
reject
require
resource
respond
   (responsibility)
restrict
   (restriction)

revolution
role
schedule
significant
similar
solar
sole
sophisticated
   (unsophis-
   ticated)
specify (specific)
statistic
style
sufficient
suppress
survive
   (survival,
   survivor)
symbol
technical
terror (terrorist)
traffic
trait
ultimate
underlie
valid
vehicle
vocabulary

Chapter 6 includes forms of the following words from the Academic and University word lists.

adequate
   (inadequate)
alternative
amendment
append
   (appendices)
benefits

bore
category
cease
civil
clause
constitute
   (constitution)

construct
cooperate
coordinate
criteria
decline
depress
dimension

dynamic
economy
   (economically)
energy
entity
grades
guarantee

index	orient	research	tradition
infrastructure	(orientation)	route	transportation
instance	percentage	schedule	trend
integrate	portion	seek	utilize
intermediate	preposition	species	version
internal	professional	status	virtual
mathematics	prospect	style	
mode	rely	technique	
motive	require	technology	

Chapter 7 includes forms of the following words from the Academic and University word lists.

academic	definite	income	research
accurate	discriminate	intelligent	(researcher)
acquire	dominate	internal	respond
adjective	emotion	interpret	(response)
apparent	emphasis	isolate	restrain
appreciate	equate	issue	rigid
(appreciation)	equipment	laboratory	series
approach	estate	lecture	simulate
arbitrary	ethic (ethical)	mature	so-called
assemble	evaluate	microscope	straightforward
attitude	exceed	modify	symbol
attribute	(excessive)	monitor	trace
(attributive)	external	passive	tradition
bulk (bulky)	factor	physical	unify
column	forthcoming	pollution	unique
complicate	fragment	(pollute)	vary (variation)
concurrent	globe	precede	violate
considerable	grade (gradable)	precise	visibly
contact	highlight	predict	vision
coordinate	ignorance	purchase	
cycle	image	range	
decline	incident	rational	

Chapter 8 includes forms of the following words from the Academic and University word lists.

academic	adjective	appreciate	attain
accumulate	aid	aspect	capable
acknowledge	alcohol	assign	category
adequate	anticipate	assist	civic

classic (classical)
clause
code
commit
   (commitment)
community
compensate
complement
complex
conceive
conflict
conform
   (conformity)
consent
convince
create (creativity)
credit
crucial
culture
decline
democracy
differentiate
divine
dominate
element
   (elementary)
emphasis

enable
encounter
enforce
err
evaluate
eventual
exceed
facilitate
focus
globe (global)
goal
heredity
immigrate
   (immigration)
imply
incidence
income
incorporate
induce
inherent
initiate
insight
instruct
   (instructor)
integral
involve
license

major
motive
   (motivate)
negative
norm
objective
occupy
passive
phase
policy
potential
precise
preposition
principal
principle
priority
proceed
prohibit
project
promote
psychology
ratio
reaction
relax
reluctant
remove
require

resolve
respond
restore
retain
revenue
revise
rigid
role
secure
seek
select
specify (specific)
statistic
strategy
submit
supplement
suppress
theory
topic
uniform
visual
vital
vocabulary
volunteer
welfare

Chapter 9 includes forms of the following words from the Academic and University word lists.

benefit
cease
commence
conjunction
converse
   (conversation)
create
duration

edit
environment
fluctuate
focus
injury
instruct.
   (instructions)
manipulate

parallel
precede
process
range
refine
reverse
structure
suspend

task
via

Chapter 10 includes forms of the following words from the Academic and University word lists.

abandon
academic
acquire
adapt
adolescent
adult
albeit
alcohol
alternatively
approach
appropriate
approximate
area
aristocrat
atmosphere
attach
bias
clause
coherence
commission
commodity
communicate
complex
compulsion
(compulsory)
compute
concentrate
conclude
(conclusion)
conduct
confer
conflict
conjunction
consequent
construct
continent
contrast
controversy
(controversial)
convene

converse
(conversation,
conversely)
create
debate
decline
demonstrate
dense
(density)
depress
despite
device
document
domestic
(domesticate)
economy
(economic)
elaborate
emotion
emphasis
(emphatically)
ensure
enumerate
environment
error
factor
fee
finance
function
fund
furthermore
globe (global)
grant
hence
identity
implement
incentive
income
indicate
injure

innovate
(innovative)
instance
integrity
intelligent
internally
issue
label
legislate
(legislature)
linguist
majority
metaphor
method
military
moist
mutual
nevertheless
nonetheless
normal
notwithstanding
nutrients
(nutritious)
odd (odds)
odor
outcome
output
overseas
oxygen
percent
portion
predict
preposition
proceed
propensity
protest
refute
register
regulate
(regulations)

reinforce
reliant
require
reside
resolve
resource
reveal
rural
saint
similar
specific
stable
starve
structure
style
subordinate
subsequent
subsidize
(subsidy)
substitute
summary
(summarize)
survive
symptom
technology
temporary
terminology
thereby
thesis
transfer
transition
transport
trivial
verbal
violate
vocabulary
voluntary
whereas
whereby
widespread

Chapter 11 includes forms of the following words from the Academic and University word lists.

access	data	invest	restrict
adjective	depress	(investment)	(restrictive)
allude	devote	journal	select
appreciate	document	(journalist)	significant
assure	edit (editor)	layer	source
(reassure)	enormous	legitimate	specify (specific)
author	expert	method	speculate
benefit	feature	minor	(speculation)
capable	file	modify	structure
chart	focus	obtain	style
clause	frustrate	parenthesis	subsidize
comment	graph	policy	survey
communicate	highlight	precede	sustain
community	huge	predict	team
compatible	identify	publish	technology
compile	impress	radical	telescope
(compilation)	incorporate	react	vary (varied)
consent	initial	reject	
contribute	instruct	rely (reliable)	
cooperate	(instructor)	research	

Chapter 12 includes forms of the following words from the Academic and University word lists.

accurate	conduct	frustrate	linguist
adequate	consent	fund	oblige
alcohol	constitute	guarantee	(obligation)
alter	(constitution)	heir	participate
analyze	consult	import	preposition
appreciate	create	income	principle
aspect	culture	individual	project
assume	deny	innovate	provoke
(assumption)	derive	(innovative)	psychology
attitude	document	institute	(psychologist)
author	edit	instructor	pursue (pursuit)
cancel	error	investigate	quote
classic (classical)	evident	(investigators)	research
colleague	(self-evident)	label	resident
complement	flexible	laboratory	(residence)
comprehend	foundation	leisure	revenue

revise
revolution
role
schedule

secure
(security)
select
(selection)

specify
stress
suppress
terminate

tradition
upsurge
volunteer

Chapter 13 includes forms of the following words from the Academic and University word lists.

academic
accurate
achieve
advocate
aesthetic
alcohol
(alcoholism)
allocate
approach
appropriate
assemble
atom (atomic)
attitude
benefit
(beneficial)
cease
circumstances
clause
client
communicate
complement
compound
comprehensive
conclude
(conclusion)
conflict
constraint
construct
consume
context
contract
convert
convince
create (creature)

crisis
culture (cultural)
currency
(current,
currently)
definite
depress
(depression)
design (designer)
diagram
dictate (dictator)
diffuse
distribute
draft
economy
eliminate
energy
(energetic)
enlighten
equipment
error
establish
finance
(financial)
focus
forgo
formula
generate
generation
goal
grade
grant
gravity
hereditary

homogeneous
hypothesis
(hypothetical)
imply
impose
impress
incident
incorporate
insist
(insistence)
institute
instruct
(instructor)
intense
interview
justify
laboratory (lab)
linguistics
maintain
(maintenance)
major
mediate
(mediator)
mental
microscope
(microscopic)
military
molecule
occur
odd
perpetrate
persist
philosophy
(philosophical)

predict
preliminary
principle
project
proportion
release
require
(requirement)
reservoir
resolve
resource
respond
(response)
restore
restrict
(restriction)
secure (security)
shrink
spontaneous
stress
submit
subsidize
suppress
synthetic
technical
tense
trait
transfer
transport
(trans-
portation)
trivial
vital

Chapter 14 includes forms of the following words from the Academic and University word lists.

accumulate	credit	issue	publication
adhere	criteria	item	purchase
adjective	culture	labor	pursue
adjust	defective	laboratory (lab)	radical
administer	depress	liable	react
advocate	detect	liberal	recover
affect	eliminate	license	repudiate
annual	emerge	major (majority)	require
anthropology	energy	manual	(requirement)
appraise	environment	mechanism	research
appropriate	equip	modify	restrict
area	estimate	monitor	(restrictive)
attain	ethical	nuclear	secure (security)
automate	evaluate	occur	seek
automatic	exclude	panel	select
benefit	export	passive	site
challenge	expose	persistence	source
channel	focus	potential	suppress
clause	fund	precede	technique
code	generation	preposition	tradition
community	goal	presume	transform
conservative	harbor	previous	transmit
consist	ideology	priority	(transmission)
constrain	instruct	process	trigger
contact	(instructor)	prohibit	undergo
context	interpret	prospect	undertake
converge	interview	(prospective)	vehicle

Chapter 15 includes forms of the following words from the Academic and University word lists.

academic	appropriate	civil (civilization)	data
achieve	area	comprise	decade
adapt	asset	compute	deprive
(adaptations)	author	conclude	diminish
adult	avail (available)	contribute	discriminate
ambiguity	benefit	(contribution)	(discrimi-
ambiguous	bomb	correspond	nation)
analyze	capable	create	dispute
apparent (appear)	(capability)	cycle	distribute

domestic
dramatic
economy
   (economics,
   economist)
efficient
   (efficiency)
eliminate
emotion
emphasis
energy
enhance
enormous
ensure
equivalent
establish
estimate
evaluate
evolve
   (evolution)
exceed
   (excessive)
explicit
finance

flexible
fulfilling
   (self-fulfilling)
generate
generation
identical
ignore
illustration
image
impact
impress
   (impressive)
incentive
indicate
insist
internal
interval
intervene
   (intervention)
intrinsic
invest
   (investment)
involve
locate (location)

logic
magnitude
maintenance
major
material
medical
medium
minor
moderate
myth
nevertheless
obvious
occur
passive
percent
perspective
physical
precise
predict
project
   (projection)
promote
qualitative
quote

react
release
research
resource
respond
   (response)
revolution
   (revolutionize)
sector
sibling
somewhat
strategy
structure
successor
   (succession)
sufficient
sum
target
tense
territory
transform
transmit
vary

Answer Key

Chapter 1

Label each word in the following (silly) story.

This	(demonstrative) pronoun
is	verb
a	(indefinite) article
very	adverb
sad	adjective
story.	noun
Jim	(proper) noun
found	verb
some	quantifier
magic	adjective
beans	noun
under	preposition
an	(indefinite) article
enormous	adjective
pile	noun
of	preposition
dirty	adjective
laundry	noun
in	preposition
his	(possessive) adjective
extremely	adverb
messy	adjective
room,	noun
but	conjunction
he	(subject) pronoun
did	auxiliary
not	adverb
want	verb
to keep	infinitive
them.	(object) pronoun
He	(subject) pronoun
gave	verb
those	(demonstrative) adjective
beans	noun
to	preposition

me,	(object) pronoun
and	conjunction
I	(subject) pronoun
put	verb
them	(object) preposition
in	preposition
a	(indefinite) article
little,	adjective
tiny	adjective
box	noun
and	conjunction
secretly	adverb
hid	verb
them	(object) pronoun
in	preposition
my	(possessive) adjective
kitchen.	noun
Our	(possessive) adjective
cat	noun
jumped	verb
into	preposition
the	(definite) article
cupboard,	noun
ate	verb
the	(definite) article
magic	adjective
beans,	noun
and	conjunction
became	verb
a	(indefinite) article
beautiful	adjective
princess.	noun
Unfortunately,	adverb
this	(demonstrative) pronoun
princess	noun
cannot	modal
speak	verb
any	quantifier
human	adjective
language.	noun
She	(subject) pronoun
meows	verb
and	conjunction
eats	verb
mice.	noun

I	(subject) pronoun
do	auxiliary verb
not	adverb
like	verb
meowing,	gerund
and	conjunction
she	(subject) pronoun
does	auxiliary verb
not	adverb
like	verb
eating	gerund
mice.	noun

Label the independent and dependent clauses and the subjects and predicates in the following sentences.

1. Pat gave a five-minute speech.   independent clause
   Pat   subject
   gave a five-minute speech   predicate
2. Urban areas have a lot of traffic,   independent clause
   Urban areas   subject
   have a lot of traffic   predicate
   but rural areas have quiet roads.   independent clause
   rural areas   subject
   have quiet roads   predicate
3. Although Ann was physically exhausted,   dependent clause
   Ann   subject
   was physically exhausted   predicate
   she continued working.   independent clause
   she   subject
   continued working   predicate
4. We appreciate the work   independent clause
   we   subject
   appreciate the work   predicate
   that Ann completed.   dependent clause
   Ann   subject
   completed   predicate
5. Sue is an intelligent student,   independent clause
   Sue   subject
   is an intelligent student   predicate
   but she failed a test   independent clause
   she   subject
   failed a test   predicate
   because she felt emotionally exhausted.   dependent clause
   she   subject
   felt emotionally exhausted   predicate

Label the subjects, verbs, direct objects, indirect objects, and complements in the following sentences.

1. Civil engineers	subject
are inspecting	verb
this bridge.	direct object
2. This bridge	subject
might collapse	verb
3. The bridge's support columns	subject
are	verb
weak.	complement
4. The bridge	subject
needs	verb
reinforcement.	direct object
5. The engineers	subject
will give	verb
the governor	indirect object
their report	direct object
6. The engineers	subject
are	verb
experts on stress in large structures.	complement

Refer to the dictionary entry for *ministry* to answer the following questions.

1. As a count noun, *ministry* means a government department. As a noncount noun, *ministry* means the work done by a religious person.
2. The phrase *the ministry* means the profession of a church leader.

Refer to the dictionary entries for *minor* to answer the following questions.

1. The adjective *minor* may be used both before nouns and in predicates.
2. In law, *minor* means someone who is below the legal age of responsibility.
3. The opposite of *minor in* is *major in*.

Chapter 2

Complete each of the following sentences with the present perfect form of the verb in parentheses. Refer to the irregular verb chart beginning on page 29 if necessary.

a. Ana HAS COMPLETED (complete) her research project on frogs.
b. She HAS WRITTEN (write) a 30-page paper.
c. Several students HAVE NOT FINISHED (not, finished) their projects yet.
d. The instructor HAS EXTENDED (extend) the deadline for completing the projects.
e. The projects HAVE TAKEN (take) more time than was expected.

Fill in each blank with an appropriate form of the verb in parentheses.

In 1891, James Naismith INVENTED (invent) the game of basketball. Naismith TAUGHT (teach) physical education at the School for Christian Workers in Springfield, Massachusetts, and bored students in the school NEEDED (need) a new indoor sport. Although Naismith SPENT (spend) most of his life teaching physical education, by the end of his life, he HAD EARNED (earn) degrees in the fields of philosophy, religion, physical education, and medicine.

Today, basketball HAS BECOME (become) an international sport. More than 300 million people around the world PLAY (play) basketball. Each year, players from many countries COMPETE (compete) for positions on professional teams in the U.S. Basketball first BECAME (become) an Olympic sport in 1936, and since then, teams from many countries HAVE PLAYED (play) against each other in international competitions.

Chapter 3

Correct the errors in the following sentences.

    a. We can assured you that the report will be ready on Friday.
       can assure   NOT can assured
    b. I could finish writing my essay for English last night.
       was able to   NOT could
    c. I don't can focus my mind on my work today.
       can't   NOT don't can
    d. This species of tree can to tolerate dry summers.
       can   NOT can to

Correct the errors in the following sentences.

    a. Sue has better cancel her appointment.
       had   NOT has
    b. Smoking should not being allowed near hospitals.
       be   NOT being
    c. Tom should obtained a schedule of classes before he tried to register for next semester.
       should have   NOT should
    d. We must to consult an attorney before we sign this contract.
       must   NOT must to
    e. Passengers don't have to take a bomb on an airplane.
       must not   NOT don't have to

Correct the errors in the following sentences.

    a. Sue should of repeated the laboratory experiments.
       should have   NOT should of
    b. She knows she not supposed to use that old data for her report.
       is not supposed to   NOT not supposed to
    c. We're not suppose to leave the lab unlocked.
       supposed   NOT suppose
    d. We had better checked the locks twice.
       check   NOT checked
    e. We should to report to the police any suspicious activities near the lab.
       should   NOT should to

Correct the errors in the following sentences.

a. Mary maybe going to attend a conference next month.
may be   NOT maybe

b. Maybe Tom happy to assist with her preparations for the conference.
Tom is happy   NOT Tom happy

c. May be the conference delegates will discuss emerging trends in education.
Maybe   NOT May be

d. Some trends may be obvious, but others maybe subtle.
may be subtle   NOT maybe subtle

Complete each of the following sentences with *maybe* or *may be.*

a. Tom MAY BE in the lab right now.
b. MAYBE he will accomplish a lot today.
c. He MAY BE working with acids.
d. Tom thinks MAYBE he will finish his project soon.

Complete each of the following sentences with *must, must have, have to,* or *had to* and a correct form of the verb in parentheses.

a. Bliss Jewelry MUST CATER (cater) to an upscale clientele. Most of their products are quite expensive.
b. Jim Taylor bought a $10,000 watch at Bliss Jewelry last week. He MUST HAVE BOUGHT (buy) it as a status symbol.
c. When he bought the watch, Jim HAD TO PAY (pay) an additional $800 in sales tax on it.
d. Now Jim MUST BE (be) very careful not to wear his watch in public places where there may be pickpockets.
e. Jim MUST THINK (think) that wearing an expensive watch will enhance his image.

Complete each of the following sentences with *could, couldn't, could have,* or *couldn't have* and an appropriate form of the verb in parentheses.

a. Our project needs greater funding. We COULD ASK (ask) for more money.
b. More money COULD SOLVE (solve) a lot of problems.
c. Last year, we COULD HAVE PREDICTED (predict) the need for a bigger budget.
d. The budget committee worked very, very hard. They COULDN'T HAVE WORKED (work) harder.
e. Last year's committee members were very skilled. All of them COULD USE (use) computer-based accounting programs.

CHAPTER 4

Complete each of the following sentences with a passive form of the given verb.

1. estimate   The number of persons with learning disabilities in the U.S. IS ESTIMATED at 15 percent of the population.
2. oblige   Schools ARE OBLIGED by federal law to provide appropriate educational opportunities for students with disabilities.
3. document   After a disability IS DOCUMENTED by a doctor or other professional, students receive special accommodation to help them succeed in school.

4. incline   In the past, schools WERE INCLINED to ignore the needs of students with disabilities.

5. label   Often in the past, people WERE LABELED "disabled" and then forgotten.

6. confine   For example, job opportunities for blind adults WERE CONFINED to special workshops for the blind.

7. couple   When educational opportunities ARE COUPLED with employment opportunities, the lives of people with disabilities become much more satisfying and fulfilling.

8. link   Work opportunities ARE LINKED to high self-esteem.

9. design   The Americans with Disabilities Act (ADA) IS DESIGNED to help all Americans participate in civic life.

10. align   The goals of the ADA ARE ALIGNED with the goals of most Americans.

Improve the following paragraph by changing the underlined sections to passive voice.

In the United States, there are laws to protect people who have permanent disabilities. <u>The rights of disabled persons are guaranteed by the Americans with Disabilities Act (ADA)</u>. However, the ADA doesn't deal with the World Wide Web. <u>The Web is accessed</u> through computer programs, and <u>many software programs have been developed</u> for persons with disabilities. Still, some information technology products have not been usable, and the government has instituted new regulations. Now, when <u>information technology products are developed</u> for the federal government, <u>these products must be made</u> accessible to persons with disabilities.

Chapter 5

Write an *E* in the blank before each sentence that contains a bare singular count noun.

  _E_ a. Jon's analysis of <u>problem</u> is weak.

  ___ b. We put gasoline in the car yesterday.

  _E_ c. Pam is a prime suspect in murder <u>case</u>.

  _E_ d. Ann does not know <u>result</u> of the laboratory experiment.

  _E_ e. The project may be slow because they are pursuing difficult <u>goal</u>.

  ___ f. Children may be harmed if they are exposed to intense violence in movies.

  _E_ g. The project will probably run into <u>complication</u> later on.

  ___ h. Children develop asthma more often when there is smog in the air.

  _E_ i. The committee reached <u>conclusion</u> that pollution is increasing.

  _E_ j. Distinctive <u>feature</u> of this car is its low price.

Edit the following sentences, correcting any errors in noun phrases. There may be more than one way to correct a sentence, and one or more sentences do not contain an error. Discuss the reasons for your choice.

  a. Jan was sole <u>survivor</u> of the accident.
    Probable correction   *the sole survivor*

  b. Please comply with <u>request</u> from the central management office.
    Some possible corrections: *requests, these requests, this request*

   c. Honesty and hard work are <u>element</u> of good business administration.
      Probable correction: *elements*

   d. It is important that <u>patient</u> consult <u>physician</u> before taking <u>drug.</u>
      Some possible corrections: *patients, a patient, the patient; a physician,*
                                     physicians, their physician; a drug, any drug, drugs,
                                       this drug

   e. If they wish to keep <u>mistake</u> to <u>minimum</u>, <u>supervisor</u> must get information to
     <u>employee</u> quickly and accurately.
      Some possible corrections: *mistakes; a minimum, the minimum; supervisors, a*
                                       supervisor, the supervisor; employees, an employee,
                                       the employee, the employees

   f. We made fundamental <u>mistake</u> at the beginning of our project.
      Some possible corrections: *a fundamental mistake, our fundamental mistake*

   g. In different <u>context</u>, this sentence would have a very different meaning.
      Probable correction: *a different context*

   h. U.S. companies import supplies from many regions.
      No correction is needed.

   i. In similar <u>way</u>, it is important to publish <u>report</u> on the environmental impact
     of <u>project</u> before the project begins.
      Probable correction: *a similar way*
      Some possible corrections: *a report, the report; a project, projects*

   j. New information will ultimately lead us to formulate new <u>hypothesis</u>.
      Some possible corrections: *new hypotheses, a new hypothesis*

Edit the following sentences, correcting any errors in noun phrases. There may be
more than one way to correct a sentence. Discuss the reasons for your choices.

   a. Philip Mazzei played crucial <u>role</u> in the American Revolution.
      Probable correction: *a crucial role*

   b. The professor raised valid <u>point</u> at committee <u>meeting</u> yesterday.
      Some possible corrections: *a valid point, several valid points; the committee*
                                         meeting, our committee meeting, a committee meeting

   c. Did Ron acquire <u>cars</u> in his garage legally?
      Probable correction: *the cars*

   d. <u>Principle</u> of marketing is that music helps sell merchandise.
      Probable correction: *a principle of marketing*

   e. There is intense magnetic <u>field</u> near the North Pole.
      Probable correction: *an intense magnetic field*

   f. <u>Critic</u> said yesterday's performance showed both intelligence and immense
     energy.
      Some possible corrections: *critics, a critic, the critic*

   g. In basketball <u>game</u>, <u>referee</u> must be neutral and not favor one team or <u>other</u>.
      Some possible corrections: *a basketball game, basketball games; referees, a referee;*
                                         the other

   h. This lecture will focus on <u>meaning</u> of statistics about population growth.
      Probable correction: *the meaning*

   i. Tax policies inhibit the growth of computer <u>company</u> in some countries.
      Probable correction: *companies*

   j. Capital is important <u>factor</u> underlying economic growth.
      Probable correction: *an important factor*

Accuracy practice
Note: It is important to check the verb forms which are used in all of these sentences.

  a. I / need / information / about / computer / code
     Key points: *information* is a noncount noun; *code* is a count noun.
  b. institution / receive / money / for research / malaria
     Key points: *institution* is a count noun; *money, research,* and *malaria* are
                   noncount nouns; *research* needs a following preposition, *on.*
  c. Lee / present / analysis / of / situation
     Key points: *analysis* and *situation* are count nouns.
  d. horizontal / axis / represent / time
     Key point: *axis* is a count noun.
  e. we / try / find / source / of / problem
     Key points: *source* and *problem* are count nouns.

Edit the following paragraph, correcting any errors in noun phrases. There is more
than one way to correct the paragraph. Discuss the reasons for your choices.

Possible correction:

     During the past decade, developments in THE computer industry have had
an immense impact on libraries. Not long ago, most libraries maintained A card
catalog of their holdings. Each time A library added A book to its collection,
someone typed A card telling THE title, author, and subject of THE book, as well
as other information. These cards were then filed alphabetically in the drawers
of A large cabinet. Library PATRONS who wished to find books on A particular
subject searched through the drawers of THE cabinet, and librarians held classes
for PATRONS teaching them how to use card CATALOGS. Such A system now
seems extremely unsophisticated. A library's holdings are now listed in A computer database. The database includes information on not only the subject,
author, and title of THE book but also its status (whether it is on THE shelves
or checked out and, if checked out, its due date). In addition, libraries now
have databases with information about ARTICLES found inside books and
JOURNALS. Librarians continue to hold classes for PATRONS, but the classes
are now about how to use COMPUTERS.

Generic use often occurs in definitions. Write definitions for the following words.

  a. hereditary trait
     Key point: *a hereditary trait is, hereditary traits are*
  b. bond
     Key point: *a bond is, bonds are*
  c. entrepreneur
     Key point: *an entrepreneur is, entrepreneurs are*
  d. contamination
     Key point: *contamination is* (noncount noun)
  e. computer
     Key point: *a computer is, computers are* (In technical writing, you may see *the
                  computer is.*)
  f. sonnet
     Key point: *a sonnet is, sonnets are*
  g. money
     Key point: *money is* (noncount noun)

Edit the following sentences, correcting any errors in noun phrases. There may be more than one way to correct a sentence. Discuss the reasons for your choices.

a. The repair crew needs accurate <u>diagram</u> of <u>plane's</u> interior.
Some possible corrections: *an accurate diagram, accurate diagrams; this plane's, the plane's*

b. The dean rejected some recommendations but accepted <u>recommendation</u> from the student committee.
Some possible corrections: *a recommendation, the recommendations, the recommendation*

c. This calculation is based on speed of light.
Probable correction: *the speed of light*

d. Store <u>manager</u> selected the winning number for <u>contest</u> at random.
Probable correction: *the store manager*
Some possible corrections: *the contest, this contest, our contest, the store's contest*

e. In particular <u>context</u>, this action may constitute a felony.
Probable correction: *a particular context*

f. There is explicit <u>rule</u> against disposing of <u>chemical</u> in the lab sinks.
Probable corrections: *an explicit rule; chemicals*

g. It is not appropriate for <u>child</u> to use motorized <u>vehicle</u>.
Some possible corrections: *a child, children; a motorized vehicle, motorized vehicles*

h. <u>Plot</u> to overthrow <u>government</u> was reported by credible news <u>agency</u> today.
Some possible corrections: *a plot, the plot, our plot; the government, our government; a credible news agency, the only credible news agency*

i. None <u>of other planets</u> in this solar system have large amounts of surface water.
Correction: *of the other planets*

Edit the following paragraphs. There may be more than one way to correct the noun phrases. Discuss the reasons for your choices.
Note: Some alternative ways of editing are in parentheses.

THE principle of free speech has been an important concept throughout THE history of THE United States. Many people argue that maintaining uninhibited free speech is crucial to maintaining our existence as A democracy and to maintaining A creative spirit within our culture. Others argue that some limits on free speech are appropriate and necessary for THE protection of individuals.

Those who advocate limits on free speech frequently cite hate speech as A (THE) category of speech that should be controlled. They argue that songs and films filled with racial insults are capable of causing significant harm to individuals and that THE glorification of violence that is found in much contemporary music is dangerous to A community (COMMUNITIES). THE Supreme Court has ruled in THE past that freedom of speech ends when it creates a clear and present danger to others. Advocates of limits maintain that singing about how good it feels to kill police or to burn down ethnic grocery stores is analogous to falsely shouting, "Fire!" in a crowded building. It is dangerous and should be illegal.

Others argue against such limits. They argue that if we place restrictions on what INDIVIDUALS are allowed to say, we run THE risk of inhibiting THE creativity of artists and of suppressing important discussions. If the government is allowed to decide what words or ideas are considered dangerous or insulting, soon any criticism of the government may be labeled "insulting" and banned. If ARTISTS are not allowed to say, write, or sing about hatred and violence, we may not find out what some people are thinking. It is better to expose negative IDEAS and argue against them than to suppress them.

Chapter 6

Accuracy practice

a. there / good news / today
   Key point: *there is*
b. there / many / alternative / routes / for commuters
   Key point: *there are*
c. there / an earlier version of this software / on / Lee / computer
   Key points: *there is/was; Lee's*
d. there / garbage / street / after / parade
   Key points: *there was/always is/will be; the/a parade, parades*
e. there / three / motive / for the crime
   Key points: *there are/were; motives*

Complete each of the following sentences with the correct form of the verb in parentheses.

a. These criteria SEEM (seem) to be important.
b. This species NEEDS (need) protection.
c. Many species ARE (be) endangered.
d. My scissors HAVE (have) blue handles.
e. A new pair of scissors IS (be) on order.

Complete each of the following sentences with the correct present tense form of the verb in parentheses.

a. Neither the intermediate students nor the advanced students USE (use) these dictionaries.
b. Either the librarian or the principal CHOOSES (choose) dictionaries for the school.
c. The teachers and the librarian WANT (want) students to utilize computer-based dictionaries.

Complete each of the following sentences with the correct form of the verb in parentheses.

a. The dimensions of the room ARE (be) quite small.
b. The size of these rooms IS (be) inadequate for our needs.
c. Some of Americans' most important civil rights ARE (be) guaranteed in the first 10 amendments to the U.S. Constitution.
d. Some of the information in this book SEEMS (seem) out of date.
e. All modes of transportation REQUIRE (require) energy.
f. The number of modes of transportation that can be supported by the infrastructure of a developing country and integrated into its internal transportation system IS (be) limited.
g. A number of scholars HAVE (have) given input on this transportation proposal.

Chapter 7

Change the following phrases into noun-noun combinations. All the phrases that you create will be common combinations.

    a. a monitor for a computer → a computer monitor
    b. a series for television → a television series
    c. the cycle of life → the life cycle
    d. a range of mountains → a mountain range
    e. a decline in the stock market → a stock market decline
    f. a symbol of status → a status symbol
    g. a tax on income → an income tax
    h. a tax on an estate → an estate tax
    i. a highlight of a movie → a movie highlight
    j. a statement of vision → a vision statement

Complete the following story with adjectives formed from the verbs in parentheses.

Sue and Tom finished cleaning the room and looked around happily at the neatly SWEPT (sweep) floor and the POLISHED (polish) wood furniture in their cozy living room. SPARKLING (sparkle) sunshine came in through the newly WASHED (wash) windows with their neatly IRONED (iron) curtains. In the kitchen, there were loaves of bread in the oven. Tom and Sue could smell the BAKING (bake) loaves and knew that soon they would eat freshly BAKED (bake) bread. The look on their SMILING (smile) faces said that they were a very happy couple.

Complete the following sentences with participial adjectives.

1. The professor's lecture confused the students. The students experienced a lot of confusion while they listened to the lecture.
    a. The lecture was very CONFUSING. It was a CONFUSING lecture.
    b. The students felt CONFUSED. They were CONFUSED students.
2. The storm frightened the children. The children felt a lot of fear.
    a. The children felt FRIGHTENED. They were very FRIGHTENED children.
    b. The storm seemed FRIGHTENING. It was a FRIGHTENING storm.
3. The news surprised the people. The people had a big surprise when they read the news.
    a. The news was quite SURPRISING. It was SURPRISING news.
    b. The people were SURPRISED. They acted like SURPRISED people.
4. Sue loves her baby very much. She gives her baby lots of love.
    a. Sue is very LOVING to her baby. She is a LOVING mother.
    b. The baby is definitely a well-LOVED child.

Complete each of the following sentences with an adjective formed from the given verb. In each case, the phrase you create will be a common collocation in English.

    1. acquire   Appreciation for lutefisk is an ACQUIRED taste.
    2. fragment Lack of coordination between government agencies resulted in a FRAGMENTED response to the problems of small communities in the mountains.
    3. justify   Community leaders are expressing a lot of JUSTIFIED anger about the government's lack of response to these problems.

4. unify   Leaders should work together and take a UNIFIED approach to problems.
5. dominate Protecting salmon is the DOMINATING concern of our organization.
6. isolate   This accident is the only one that has happened, so I think it is an ISOLATED incident.
7. pollute   Fish can't live in a POLLUTED stream.
8. restrain The judge issued a RESTRAINING order to stop people from polluting the river.
9. assemble Dr. Lee discussed the judge's order with the ASSEMBLED group.
10. predict Our publicity campaign did not meet with the PREDICTED response, because no one listened to our ads.

Complete each of the following sentences with a correct form of the modifier in parentheses.

a. The president's approach to the problem was SIMPLER THAN (simple) the mayor's approach.
b. The president's approach was MORE STRAIGHTFORWARD THAN (straightforward) the mayor's approach.
c. The mayor's suggestion was THE MOST COMPLICATED (complicated) of all the suggestions.
d. My suggestion is AS GOOD AS (good) the mayor's suggestion.
e. The mayor's idea is THE WORST (bad) idea that I have ever heard.
f. I am AS INTELLIGENT AS (intelligent) the mayor.

Use the data in the table to complete the following sentences. Use adverbs to modify the comparisons.

1. The Jaguar is SLIGHTLY (MARGINALLY, MINIMALLY) LESS EXPENSIVE THAN (expensive) the Land Rover.
2. The Dodge is DEFINITELY (OBVIOUSLY, DRAMATICALLY) CHEAPER THAN (cheap) the Lexus.
3. The Dodge is APPRECIABLY (CONSIDERABLY) CHEAPER THAN (cheap) the Ford.
4. The Lexus is CONSIDERABLY (APPRECIABLY) MORE EXPENSIVE THAN (expensive) the Cadillac.

Chapter 8

Accuracy practice

a. we / anticipate / complete / first phase / the project / next week
   Key points: *anticipate completing; the first phase*
b. yesterday / Jon / finish / one job / and / proceed / start / another
   Key points: *finished; proceeded to start*
c. Internet / facilitate / find / facts / quickly
   Key points: *the Internet; facilitates finding*
d. driver of the car / acknowledge / exceed / speed limit
   Key points: *the driver; acknowledged exceeding; the speed limit*
e. Dr. Nye / consent / speak on / theory / global warming
   Key points: *consented to speak; her/his/the theory of*

Chapter 9

Use parallel structure to improve the following sentences.

a. The temperature here fluctuates between a low of 35°F and the highest temperature, which is 95°F.
The temperature here fluctuates between a low of 35°F and a high of 95°F.

b. The duration of treatment for this type of injury ranges between six weeks and half of a year.
The duration of treatment for this type of injury ranges between six weeks and six months.

c. Sue doesn't give her children foods that are processed, refined, or have a coating of sugar on them.
Sue doesn't give her children foods that are processed, refined, or sugarcoated.

d. Tom's profits from running his business were offset by losses from the stocks that he sold.
Tom's profits from running his business were offset by losses from selling stocks.

e. This skin cream will heal acne, prevent you from getting sunburned, and reverse the effects of aging.
This skin cream will heal acne, prevent sunburn, and reverse the effects of aging.

f. Babies explore their environment by manipulating objects and put the objects in their mouths.
Babies explore their environment by manipulating objects and putting them in their mouths.

Chapter 10

Correct the punctuation mistakes in the following sentences.

a. Ron is unhappy in his new school. Because he doesn't adapt well to new situations.
Ron is unhappy in his new school because . . .

b. Cactus plants are adapted to dry climates, therefore, they survive in deserts.
Cactus plants are adapted to dry climates; therefore, . . .
or *Cactus plants are adapted to dry climates. Therefore, . . .*

c. Jan attaches labels to all of her computer disks. So that she doesn't lose them.
Jan attaches labels to all of her computer disks so that . . .

d. Ann sent an attachment with her e-mail, however, Tom didn't know how to open it.
Ann sent an attachment with her e-mail; however, . . .
or *Ann sent an attachment with her e-mail. However, . . .*

e. Sue is emotionally attached to her old toys, consequently, she doesn't want to give them away.
Sue is emotionally attached to her old toys. Consequently, . . .
or *Sue is emotionally attached to her old toys; consequently, . . .*

Underline the transitional words and expressions in the following, brief essay. Notice the function of each one, indicated at the right margin.

In the history of the world, several languages have been used for international communication, but there has never before been one language that could be used all around the world. Today, English is becoming a global language because of economic factors.	(thesis)
Some people say that English isn't spoken widely enough to be called a global language. <u>Granted</u>, the majority of people in the world don't speak English. <u>Even so</u>, English is spoken all around the world.	concession
Other people think that English has become a global language because it has a simple grammar and a large vocabulary. Linguists disagree. They tell us that all languages are complex and that all languages can express any idea.	refutation
There are three main reasons English is becoming a global language. <u>First</u>, historically, the economic power of English-speaking nations spread English around the world. In the 18th and 19th centuries, Britain established colonies in many parts of the world.	sequence
<u>Then</u>, in the 20th century, the military and economic power of the United States ensured the widespread use of English. <u>As a result</u>, English is spoken on every continent on the globe.	sequence result
<u>Second</u>, many people believe that they can get better jobs if they learn English, both <u>because</u> most international business is conducted in English and <u>because</u> many multinational corporations use English as their language of internal communication. For many people, learning English has become an important step toward professional advancement.	sequence cause
<u>Lastly</u>, English is used for a large part of Internet communication. Approximately 80 percent of Web pages are in English. <u>Consequently</u>, people want to learn English so they can find information on the Web.	sequence result
<u>In brief</u>, many factors are influencing the spread of English. Economic forces of the past (colonies and trade), present (international business), and future (widespread use of the Internet) are making English a global language.	summary (thesis)

Fill each blank in the following brief essay with a suitable word or phrase from this list: *because, finally, first, for example, for instance, in conclusion, nevertheless, nonetheless, in contrast, secondly, therefore, third, to summarize, unless.* Use each expression in the list only once. You will not need to use every expression in the list.

Many families own pets. Pets provide comfort and companionship, and one of the most enjoyable pets is a cat. In fact, <u>because</u> cats have many fine qualities, every family should think about acquiring a cat.	cause
Granted, cats are not perfect. Cats have propensities toward killing songbirds and bringing dead mice into the house. <u>Nevertheless/Nonetheless</u>, there are many good reasons to own a cat.	concession and contrast

<u>First</u>, cats are simple to care for. <u>For example/For instance</u>, cats keep themselves clean. One very rarely has to bathe a cat.	sequence example
Dogs, <u>in contrast</u>, develop foul odors if they aren't bathed regularly.	contrast
<u>Secondly</u>, cats don't make a lot of noise <u>unless</u> they are in danger. <u>For example/For instance</u>, if a dog attacks a cat, the cat may yowl. Likewise, if a person steps on a cat's tail, the cat may hiss quite loudly.	sequence condition example
<u>Third</u>, cats are pleasurable to watch. Ever since cats were domesticated by the ancient Egyptians, people have admired cats' aristocratic good looks and graceful movements.	sequence
<u>To summarize/In conclusion</u>, cats are easy to care for, quiet, and beautiful. <u>Therefore</u>, everyone should consider owning a cat.	conclusion result

Chapter 11

Rewrite each of the following sentences, making a subject adjective clause from the clause in parentheses.

a. Lee bought an insurance policy (the policy covers earthquake damage to his home).
   Lee bought an insurance policy that covers earthquake damage to his home.
b. The graph (the graph shows how much the policy will pay) is on page 3.
   The graph that shows how much the policy will pay is on page 3.
c. An earthquake (the earthquake measures 6.0 on the Richter scale) is capable of causing serious structural damage to buildings.
   An earthquake that measures 6.0 on the Richter scale is capable of causing serious structural damage to buildings.
d. The insurance agent (the insurance agent sold Lee the policy) said that many people are buying these policies.
   The insurance agent who sold Lee the policy said that many people are buying these policies.
e. Scientists (the scientists study earthquakes) predict that Seattle will experience a very severe earthquake in the future.
   Scientists who study earthquakes predict that Seattle will experience a very severe earthquake in the future.

Rewrite each of the following sentences, making an object adjective clause from the clause in parentheses.

a. Pam edited the report (Tim wrote the report).
   Pam edited the report that Tim wrote.
b. The concern (people feel the concern) about earthquakes is legitimate.
   The concern that people feel about earthquakes is legitimate.
c. Information (scientists obtained the information from studying previous earthquakes) suggests that Seattle is very vulnerable to earthquakes.
   Information that scientists obtained from studying previous earthquakes suggests that Seattle is very vulnerable to earthquakes.
d. Scientists will soon publish the new evidence (they have acquired the evidence).
   Scientists will soon publish the new evidence that they have acquired.

e. Much of the information about future earthquakes (newspapers publish the information) is actually just speculation.
Much of the information about future earthquakes that newspapers publish is actually just speculation.

Rewrite each of the following sentences, making a preposition adjective clause from the clause in parentheses.

a. The article (the professor commented on the article) was published last week.
The article that the professor commented on was published last week.
or *The article on which the professor commented was published last week.*

b. The information (you are looking for the information) can be found on the Web.
The information that you are looking for can be found on the Web.
or *The information for which you are looking can be found on the Web.*

c. The report (this data will be incorporated into the report) is due in March.
The report that this data will be incorporated into is due in March.
or *The report into which this data will be incorporated is due in March.*

Combine each of the following sets of clauses into one sentence, making an adjective clause using *where* or *when* from the clause in parentheses.

a. Seattle is a city. (People drink a lot of coffee there.)
Seattle is a city where people drink a lot of coffee.

b. The town was quite small. (I was born in the town.)
The town where I was born was quite small.

c. There was a time. (People always knew their neighbors.)
There was a time when people always knew their neighbors.

d. I want to find a time and date. (We can meet at that time and date.)
I want to find a time and date when we can meet.

Combine each of the following sets of clauses into one sentence, making an adjective clause using *whose* from the clause in parentheses.

a. Ann is an author. (Her books sell very well in Europe.)
Ann is an author whose books sell very well in Europe.)

b. Ted is a journalist. (We respect his work.)
Ted is a journalist whose work we respect.

c. Lee attends a school. (The school's founder was Thomas Jefferson.)
Lee attends a school whose founder was Thomas Jefferson.

Combine each of the following sets of clauses into one sentence, making an adjective clause using *of which* or *of whom* from the clause in parentheses.

a. Emily Dickinson produced a large body of poetry. (Much of her poetry remained unpublished during her lifetime.)
Emily Dickinson produced a large body of poetry, much of which remained unpublished during her lifetime.

b. Now her poems are appreciated by thousands of people. (Many of the people memorize them in school.)
Now her poems are appreciated by thousands of people, many of whom memorize them in school.

   c. A complete compilation of Dickinson's poems was published in 1955. (The editor of the compilation was Thomas Johnson.)
     A complete compilation of Dickinson's poems was published in 1955, the editor of which was Thomas Johnson.

Chapter 12

Correct the errors in the following sentences.

   a. I know where is the library.
     where the library is   NOT where is the library
   b. What Les and Tim are studying are important.
     is important   NOT are important
   c. Lee is involved in research on how much leisure time do Americans have now.
     time Americans have now   NOT time do Americans have now

Accuracy practice

   a. how / AIDS virus / suppress / immune system / be / not / fully / understood
     Key points: *the AIDS virus; suppresses; the immune system; is*
   b. why / there / upsurge / volcanic activity / be / subject / research
     Key points: *an upsurge in; is; a subject for, the subject of*
   c. what / psychologist / discover / be / quite / interesting
     Key points: *psychologists, this/a psychologist; is*
   d. which / projects / will / succeed / be / difficult / predict
     Key points: *is; to predict*
   e. when / investigators / finish / is / unknown
     Key points: *the investigators; will finish, finished*

Change the following sentences into sentences with *it* as the subject.

   1. That volunteering is an important part of American culuture is well documented.
     It is well documented that volunteering is an important part of American culture.
   2. That volunteering increases with income is clear.
     It is clear that volunteering increases with income.
   3. That many low-income individuals also volunteer each week surprises some people.
     It surprises some people that many low-income individuals also volunteer each week.

Read the following direct quotation and then complete the four sentences that follow.

Answers will vary. Some possible answers are as follows.

   1. Jan said that she had often used the Internet to research volunteer organizations.
   2. She specified that she had used the Habitat for Humanity Web site.
   3. She also reported that she had searched the Internet for information on volunteer opportunities.
   4. Finally, she stated that she was hoping to find a project she could participate in somewhere near her home.

Chapter 13

Accuracy practice

    a. if / two / atom / combine / form / molecule
       Key points: *atoms; they form; a molecule*
    b. if / have / difficult / goal / must / work / hard
       Key points: *a difficult goal; must work*
    c. government / will / respond / if / military threat
       Key points: *the government; there is; a military threat*

The following sentences express hypothetical situations. Fill in the blanks in each sentence with appropriate verb forms from the words in parentheses.

    a. I am extremely tired today. I don't want to do anything. If I FELT (feel) a little more energetic, I WOULD START (start) work on my paper for my philosophy class.
    b. The Alpha Corporation does not allow any kind of flextime for its workers. A lot of workers are leaving for other companies. If the corporation HAD (have) a more enlightened attitude, it WOULD NOT LOSE (not lose) so many qualified workers.
    c. Ann doesn't understand the gravity of the situation. If she WERE TOLD (tell) how serious the problem is, she WOULD RESPOND (respond) more appropriately.
    d. The Gamma Corporation has very few security rules and no security officers. They WOULD HAVE (have) fewer thefts if they INSTITUTED (institute) more elaborate security precautions.

Accuracy practice

    a. if / population / be / homogeneous / marketing / be / easier
       Key points: *the population were; marketing would be*
    b. if / company / face / financial / crisis / bank / might / lend / money
       Key points: *the company faced; a financial crisis; the/their/a bank; might lend it*
    c. I / not / worry / if / I / be / you
       Key points: *would not worry; I were*
    d. production method / be / popular / if / it / not / consume / so much / energy
       Key points: *this/our/the production method; would be; did not consume*
    e. people / get / help / if / public / have / enlightened attitude / toward alcoholism
       Key points: *would get; the public had; an enlightened attitude*

The following sentences express hypotheses about the past. Complete each sentence with appropriate verb forms from the words in parentheses.

    a. If the designers of these offices HAD USED (use) less intense colors, they WOULD HAVE ACHIEVED (achieve) more aesthetically pleasing results.
    b. Authorities are not convinced that the riot was spontaneous. If it HAD BEEN (be) spontaneous, there WOULD NOT HAVE BEEN (not be) so many signs of communication between leaders on different streets.

c. If the local government HAD NOT IMPOSED (not impose) severe restrictions on development some years ago, most of the farmland around here WOULD HAVE BEEN CONVERTED (convert) into housing developments and shopping malls.

d. There WOULD NOT HAVE BEEN (not be) so many complaints from employees if the workload HAD BEEN DISTRIBUTED (distribute) more equitably.

e. The courts WOULD HAVE RULED (rule) in their favor if they HAD HAD (have) a justified complaint, but they didn't.

Accuracy practice

a. if / professor / draw / better / diagram / yesterday / I / understand / problem
   Key points: *the/my/our professor had drawn; a better diagram; would have understood; the problem*

b. if / committee / assemble / necessary information / earlier / they / finish / report / last week
   Key points: *the/our committee; had assembled; the necessary information; would have finished; the/their/our report*

c. reporter / be granted / interview / yesterday / if / submit / written request
   Key points: *the/this reporter; would have been granted; an interview; he/she had submitted; a written request*

d. mayor / not / be reelected / if / she / advocate / increased taxes / last year
   Key points: *the/our mayor; would not have been; had advocated*

e. if / companies / accept / government mediator / conflict / be solved / quickly
   Key points: *the companies; had accepted; a government mediator; the/this conflict; would have been solved*

The following sentences express hypothetical conditionals in mixed time. Complete each sentence with appropriate verb forms from the words in parentheses.

a. If Don HAD NOT TAKEN (not take) his wife for granted, he WOULD STILL BE (still be) a married man.

b. This project WOULD HAVE BEEN (be) completed by now if the Office of Development HAD NOT INSISTED (not insist) on reviewing our plans in microscopic detail before we began working.

c. If the developers of this program HAD TAKEN (take) even rudimentary precautions against fraud, we WOULD NOT BE FACING (not face) the problems we do now.

d. If the Lambda Corporation HAD NOT BUILT (not build) such a reservoir of goodwill in the community, their current public relations problems WOULD BE (be) much more serious.

e. If the federal government HAD NOT SUBSIDIZED (not subsidize) so much housing in the 1980s, communities WOULD BE DEALING (deal) with a much larger homeless population today.

The following sentences contain hidden conditionals. Rewrite them as conditional sentences using *if*.

a. This contract requires us to use all natural fabrics. Otherwise, we would use synthetic fabrics here.
If this contract did not require us to use all natural fabrics, we would use synthetic fabrics here.

b. In a more homogeneous group, we could reach an agreement more quickly.
If this were a more homogeneous group, we could reach an agreement more quickly.

c. In the event that this rain persists, we will forgo our plans for a picnic.
If this rain persists, we will forgo our plans for a picnic.

d. The city allocates a very small proportion of its budget to park maintenance. Under other circumstances, we would be able to replant the flower beds each year.
If the city did not allocate a very small proportion of its budget to park maintenance, we would be able to replant the flower beds each year.

e. With a more philosophical approach to his problems, he could have avoided a lot of stress.
If he had had (had taken) a more philosophical approach to his problems, he could have avoided a lot of stress.

Fill in the blanks in the following sentences, then write two or three more sentences to complete each paragraph. Use implied conditional forms.

a. It's hard to imagine what the modern world WOULD be like without private automobiles. Without this form of personal transportation, . . .

b. I hate to think what life WOULD be like without doctors, hospitals, and other forms of modern medical care. Under those circumstances, . . .

Correct the errors in the following sentences.

a. This contract requires that the stream behind the construction site is restored to its original condition.
be restored   NOT is restored

b. The employees' union continues to demand that employees aren't required to work more than six hours of overtime a week.
not be required   NOT aren't required

c. The directors' insistence that the company transfers its accounts to a new bank was not welcome news to its current bank.
tranfer   NOT transfers

d. The clients asked that the architect incorporated a home office into the plans for their house.
incorporate   NOT incorporated

e. It is imperative that the dispute between the city council and the firefighters' union is resolved.
be resolved   NOT is resolved

For each of the following sentences, compose a new sentence that expresses a wish for the opposite situation.

a. Learning English takes a lot of time and energy.
   I wish that learning English didn't take a lot of time and energy.
b. Our decisions are dictated by financial constraints.
   I wish that our decisions weren't dictated by financial constraints.
c. The director will make a lot of announcements.
   I wish the director wouldn't make a lot of announcements.
d. This report was released to the press yesterday.
   I wish this report had not been released to the press yesterday.
e. Discretionary funds were eliminated from the budget.
   I wish discretionary funds had not been eliminated from the budget.

Accuracy practice

a. Lee / hope / that / work / impress / boss
   Key points: *hopes; this/his work; will impress; the/his boss*
b. I / wish / that / all / dictator / resign from office
   Key points: *dictators; would resign*
c. we / wish / that / we / eliminate / disease
   Key point: *could eliminate*
d. I / wish / war / cease
   Key point: *would/could cease*
e. tomorrow / Sue / wish / she / not / spend / money / today
   Key points: *will wish; had not spent*
f. Kim / wish / atomic / weapon / not / be / invent
   Key points: *wishes; atomic weapons; had not been invented*

Complete each of the following sentences with the appropriate forms of the verb in parentheses.

a. Tom wishes he HAD BOUGHT (buy) a microscope last month.
b. I wish the economy HAD BEEN (be) stronger last year.

Chapter 14

Underline the participial phrases in the following sentences. What do they mean? (There may be more than one correct way to interpret a phrase.)

a. All rules <u>affecting students</u> are posted in the library.
b. Students must sign a note <u>acknowledging their acceptance of these rules</u>.
c. Students <u>accumulating more than $25.00 in fines</u> will lose library privileges.
d. Any student <u>not adhering to these rules</u> may be dismissed from school.
e. Students <u>damaging school property</u> are liable for the cost of repairs.

Underline the participial phrases in the following sentences. What do they mean? (There may be more than one correct way to interpret a phrase.)

a. This book contains poems <u>written by high school students</u>.
b. It is an annual publication <u>devoted to student writing</u>.
c. The stories and poems <u>selected by the editors</u> represent the best of student writing.
d. The editors use a selection process <u>considered very fair to students</u>.
e. The decisions <u>made by a panel of judges</u> are final.

Complete each of the following sentences with a present or past participial form of the verb in parentheses.

a. Nuclear power generation, ADVOCATED (advocate) by the leaders of several developing nations, presents many safety issues.

b. Many of the problems CONFRONTING (confront) the nuclear power industry seem almost unsolvable.

c. Regulations ADMINISTERED (administer) by the Department of Energy cover the training of workers in power plants.

d. The damage CAUSED (cause) by the Chernobyl nuclear accident transformed a large part of Ukraine into a wasteland.

e. Radiation RELEASED (release) into the air at Chernobyl was detected by monitors in Sweden.

f. Information about the explosion, SUPPRESSED (suppress) in the first weeks after the accident, later came to light.

g. Areas SELECTED (select) for processing nuclear waste are usually far away from population centers.

h. Sites ELIMINATED (eliminate) from consideration include any place where earthquakes have occurred.

i. New techniques for storing nuclear waste, DEVELOPED (develop) in university research labs, may make nuclear power production safer.

Combine each of the following pairs of sentences into one sentence in two different ways. First, use an adjective clause. Then, use a participial phrase.

a. Our home has an automated alarm system. It was installed by Kappa Security.
Our home has an automated alarm system that was installed by Kappa Security.
Our home has an automated alarm system installed by Kappa Security.

b. The system is very high tech. It consists of lights and a siren.
The system, which consists of lights and a siren, is very high tech.
The system, consisting of lights and a siren, is very high tech.

c. The system automatically contacts Kappa Security. It is triggered by sound or motion.
The system, which is triggered by sound or motion, automatically contacts Kappa Security.
The system, triggered by sound or motion, automatically contacts Kappa Security.

d. Personnel monitor the system 24 hours a day. They work in the head office.
Personnel who work in the head office monitor the system 24 hours a day.
Personnel working in the head office monitor the system 24 hours a day.

e. A code word activates the system. The code word is entered on a control panel.
A code word, which is entered on a control panel, activates the system.
A code word, entered on a control panel, activates the system.

Combine each of the following pairs of sentences into one sentence by making the first sentence in each pair into a participial phrase.

a. Pam was exposed to liberal political thinking when she was a child. She joined a radical pollitical party when she began her university studies.
Exposed to liberal political thinking when she was a child, Pam joined a radical political party when she began her university studies.
or *Having been exposed to liberal political thinking when she was a child, . . .*

b. Pam dedicated the majority of her time to political activities. She emerged
   as a leader of her party.
   *Dedicating the majority of her time to political activities, Pam emerged as a leader of
   her party.*
c. Pam attained a leadership position. She then decided she didn't agree with
   her party's ideas.
   *Having attained a leadership position, Pam then decided she didn't agree with her
   party's ideas.*
d. Pam repudiated her liberal political ideology. She joined a conservative
   political party.
   Repudiating her liberal political ideology, Pam joined a conservative political party.
   or *Having repudiated her liberal political ideology, . . .*
e. Pam was welcomed into the conservative party. She channeled her energy
   into organizing fund-raising dinners.
   *Welcomed into the conservative party, Pam channeled her energy into organizing
   fund-raising dinners.*

Rewrite the following sentences, using a participial phrase instead of an adverb clause.

a. Because she enjoys challenges, Ann frequently undertakes new projects.
   Enjoying challenges, . . .
b. While she was attending college, Ann ran a small business.
   While attending college, . . .
c. When she is considering a new business venture, Ann always evaluates its
   potential for profit.
   When considering a new business venture, . . .
d. Before she purchased her flower shop, she estimated its potential sales
   volume.
   Before purchasing her flower shop, . . .
e. Since she purchased the shop, she has constantly tried to improve it.
   Since purchasing the shop, . . .